Welfare

Key Concepts series

Welfare

Mary Daly

polity

First edition published in 2001 by Polity Press
This edition first published in 2011 by Polity Press

Polity Press
65 Bridge Street
Cambridge CB2 1UR, UK

Polity Press
350 Main Street
Malden, MA 02148, USA

ISBN-13: 978-0-7456-4470-7
ISBN-13: 978-0-7456-4471-4(pb)

A catalogue record for this book is available from the British Library.

Typeset in 10.5 on 12 pt Sabon
by Toppan Best-set Premedia Limited
Printed and bound in Great Britain by MPG Books Group Limited, Bodmin, Cornwall

For further information on Polity, visit our website: www.politybooks.com

Contents

Acknowledgements

I offer my thanks to all those who helped me with the writing of this book. In particular, I thank Barbara MacLennan and David Purdy for their excellent feedback just at the time when it was most needed. I would also like to thank the reviewers for their helpful and thought-provoking comments (and especially the reviewer who read the document a second time). I also thank my colleagues and Head at the School of Sociology, Social Policy and Social Work at Queen's University for their collegiality and support. I owe a debt also to Dennis Hogan and the Department of Sociology at Brown University for providing me with a friendly base from which to conduct my research on the US. Finally, it is a pleasure to acknowledge the guidance and support I received from staff at Polity Press. Emma Longstaff helped especially in the early days when I was trying to put the idea for the book together and Jonathan Skerrett was extremely supportive and gave invaluable guidance throughout.

Lists of Tables, Figures and Boxes

List of Tables

List of Figures

List of Boxes

Introduction

This book presents an account and analysis of welfare as a concept and a focus of political and social organisation. It traces welfare's history in academic work and considers different applications and forms of welfare in relation to everyday life. The book is especially interested in offering a social reflection on welfare – this directs it towards the social relations of welfare. Welfare is an old idea, with deep roots in a number of disciplines. In academic work it has a specific history, referring to the satisfactions yielded by economic transactions, or to an ideal form of ethical and political functioning, or to a condition of meeting need and addressing social problems. Welfare has a more general set of uses and applications also. Expressed in popular accounts, it connotes well-being in the sense of having our needs and desires met. All usages of the term tend to have a strong moral content: welfare engages not just with how we ourselves live but with how we think others should live as well. This may be assessed in relation to standards and functioning of everyday life or, more abstractly, in terms of whether and how principles such as equality, justice and liberty are esteemed. There are thorny questions and decisions involved, pertaining to how resources should be shared out, the meaning of community and belonging, and the extent to which individuals, groups and governments have social responsibilities. In effect, welfare rests on contested terrain.

Welfare-related issues have never been more relevant. The kinds of challenge faced by societies are common in several respects: How can welfare be secured in a context of decreasing resources and threats to ecological survival? How are the rising expectations of the populace to be met when decisions about resources seem to be shaped more and more by discourses of scarcity and blame? The changing context predates the latest recession. What one might call 'the democratic social settlement' in Europe and other highly industrialised parts of the world – based on the implicit promise of a good job, an improving standard of living, and the security of a peaceful unfolding of a lifetime of achievement and progress – has been coming under increasing pressure for at least a decade or more. And, of course, the last two years of crisis in the global financial and political systems have heightened insecurities massively. However, the erosion of key institutions set in before 2008. Rising levels of poverty and inequality indicate that what we thought were well-established mechanisms of security and mobility – arrangements providing a guarantee of an autonomous future to each generation – have not been as effective in recent decades as they once were.

There are many insecurities. The European Union (EU) undertook in 2007 a consultation on and investigation of the factors making for change and insecurity in the member countries.[1]

It highlighted the following as of most concern to people:

- Economic opportunity and the changing nature of work
- Ageing society, demography and changed family life, gender issues
- Poverty and inequality
- Education and mobility
- Quality of life, including climate change
- Health
- Crime and anti-social behaviour
- Migration, diversity and multi-culturalism.

It seems like there are two aspects to people's insecurities. On the one hand, what we have come to regard as the great 'integrators' – the family, school/college, employment, the social security system – are struggling. The family is much more subject to change throughout the life course than it used to be; school and education no longer guarantee advancement and social mobility; having a job no longer means a progressive career and a way of staying out of poverty; and social protection cannot be counted on to deliver a secure retirement pension or income substitute when one cannot be employed. There is a second aspect to insecurity also which relates to feelings of belonging, especially in the context of increasingly diverse societies. People are conscious of profound differences and they can readily identify a range of inter-group tensions in their society. In a survey carried out in the EU in 2007, some 40 per cent of people perceived a 'lot of tension' between ethnic or racial groups, 31 per cent saw strong tensions existing between religious groups, and around a third viewed the relationship between rich and poor and between management and workers as fraught (Rose and Newton 2010). Another way of putting all of this is to say that the 'we' is less likely to include the mass of citizens. People are more likely to break themselves up into smaller groups and to view themselves in opposition to 'them'. Lister (2004) refers to this as a process of 'othering', wherein we put a distance, barriers even, between ourselves and those whom we consider 'different' or unwelcome.

Welfare, however defined, is part of all of this. Even in the debate on the current recession, certain elements of relevance to welfare emerge as non-negotiable. While it is assumed that the government will step in to relieve the banks, businesses and maybe even mortgage holders, efforts to help alleviate (or 'bail out' as per common parlance) should not jeopardise general welfare. It seems that some state welfare-conferring activities are taken for granted. The question of 'whose welfare?' is controversial though. For example, the bailout of the banks and the general failure to change the highly self-interested nature of corporate culture is counterposed to the general welfare of society. Even though it may not always have a sharp focus, there is a sense of a generalised welfare which pits the 'common man' against the elite. Relative power and powerlessness are an important part of the sub-text here.

As mentioned, welfare is an old idea. But it has not been prominent in recent scholarship – no one argues for welfare anymore (or not explicitly anyway). I attribute this to three main factors. First, the word or term has acquired negative overtones, especially in the US. It has come to be associated with 'dependency' and perceived behavioural dysfunction on the part of those who are seen to prefer to claim benefits rather than work. This (very particular) set of meanings has proceeded to influence understandings of the term in other countries as well. A second set of reasons for why welfare has fallen out of favour has to do with its perceived lack of fit with today's highly developed society. With some core references to subsistence and financial sufficiency, welfare is seen to pertain to an earlier state of societal development. Its rudimentary connotations are considered to render the concept inappropriate for richer societies where, for example, people organise their lives in a more individualised fashion and yearn for self-realisation and fulfilment. This leads to a third possible objection to the concept – that it is out of fashion. In societies which strive after the optimum rather than the minimum and where questions of identity, subjectivity and the quality of personal relationships dominate, welfare seems to miss the mark. Hence, concepts like well-being, happiness and quality of life have come to eclipse welfare in that 'space' wherein satisfaction of needs and conditions of existence are elucidated. It is somewhat ironic that new scholarship has problematised some of the issues contained in the concept of welfare but it has not used the concept of welfare to do so.

Part of the book's aim is to explore the landscape within which welfare as a concept has fallen from view. We shall examine the different origins of welfare and show which concepts are leading proximate scholarship now and what it is about them which seems to better capture aspects of contemporary life and aspiration. Reflecting critically on this, we shall see that the concept of welfare possesses an important set of resonances that are downgraded by some of the newer concepts. Welfare's strong suit includes, for example, its references to sufficiency of material resources, the general allocation and distribution of resources, the nature of people's life chances and the role of the state and other institutions in economic and social life. These can confer powerful insights given that we still know too little about people's chances of welfare and the linkages between the activities and relations that people engage in and the mechanisms put in place by the state and other institutions around welfare-related goals. However, the concept of welfare also has weaknesses or blind sides that constitute strengths of some of the new scholarship. It leaves important questions unpressed, including issues around subjective and relational aspects of welfare. What about people's felt well-being and the connections between a person's personal life and objective situation? What about the relations one is involved in? Some kind of opening up of the concept is therefore necessary and so we nudge loose welfare's original set of references in order to take account of some of the more social and relational elements. This is rich terrain.

The book is in many ways an account and interpretation of responses to changes in social, political and economic organisation. It aims to show that, in a period of deep-reaching change, the concept of welfare, construed in a complex way, gives access to important analyses and arguments about public policy, ethical principles and the organisation of economic, political and social life. To put it otherwise: the concept helps to provide ways of understanding the connection between welfare-related rationales and institutions as they are embedded at a systemic level, especially in social policies and programmes, and the resources and levels of well-being that people obtain in real life. With this in mind, the book updates the register of thinking about welfare. It does so in a threefold manner: how welfare is conceived and discussed, how it is politicised, and how it is a feature of the organisation of everyday life. This leads us to engage with academic work, policy and political thought and discourse, and the empirical everyday world. Two core questions drive this book. The first asks how are we to understand welfare as it developed through scholarship historically and as it is reflected in contemporary theorising and research. The second queries the constituents of welfare viewed in terms of real lives in contemporary times, focusing on people's agency and how this links with and is shaped by actions on the part of the state, market-based interests, the family and community.

Definition and Focus

In terms of definition, welfare as conceived of here refers to a set of ideals and practices characterising human behaviour across a variety of sites: state, family, community, market. It is seen to have application at micro and macro levels (which is one of the concept's strengths to be developed in this book) and may be conceptualised as a point where micro- and macro-level processes meet. At the micro level of everyday life, welfare is conceived in terms of the comparative levels of resources enjoyed by people, individually and collectively, and the activities engaged in around securing important resources. While the prime focus is on material resources, a comprehensive definition of welfare must also include people's social relations and their levels and types of participation in a range of activities. This is the social welfare interest of the book: welfare as fashioned by social practices and social relations. It will be obvious that when we use the term 'welfare' in this book, we mean something very different to the negative and confined sense of the term's usage in the US.

Welfare has to be located also as part of a system of social and institutional relationships through which a collective infrastructure and set of social arrangements is put in place. So while individuals 'construct' key aspects of their own welfare, they do so in a context where societies actively 'organise' and 'reorganise' for welfare conceived in a more collective manner (O'Brien and Penna 1998: 7–8). To put this another way, for the purposes of this book people are seen as active in searching after or securing 'welfare' but their options and behaviour are constrained or empowered structurally. Policy and provision are closely involved here. Therefore, an analysis of state activity (in terms of discourse, architecture and provision) is a central part of the exercise of identifying the nature and structuring of welfare in contemporary societies. The third sense or level at which welfare is conceptualised in this book is as part of an academic discourse, the subject of thinking and research through which knowledge about and meanings of welfare are produced and legitimated. Welfare in this meaning refers to a body of knowledge located in ideology and culture. And so, rather than treating academic conceptions of welfare as a neutral, scientific store of learning, we see them as political (in the sense of carrying forward particular interests) and contested.

In its conceptualisation, the book follows and builds upon a distinction made by O'Brien and Penna (1998: 7–8) between the academic discursive, the systemic, and the experiential aspects of welfare. These give the book its structure. We start with the academic, with welfare as an idea or set of ideas in academic work. The second part considers welfare in political discourse and as a focus of political organisation – its subject is on the one hand welfare in political thought and on the other the organisation of welfare by political institutions (especially the state). The level of practice – the 'doing' of welfare – is the subject of the book's third part. While the guiding empirical interest here is in how people fare in putting together their livelihoods, life courses and relations, space and information limitations mean that we can really set out only the contours here. It should be seen as an exercise in exploring particular contexts in which welfare is operating. We look at 'welfare in action' in two areas: the labour market and the family and community. We are interested in identifying the structure and opportunities put in place for people rather than specific hard and fast outcomes.

A crucial link to be clarified at this stage is that of welfare and the welfare state. These are often elided but not in this book. While welfare states are one of the most important institutions for effecting welfare (especially in Europe and other highly developed regions), welfare cannot and should not be equated with the welfare state. The welfare state has no monopoly on welfare. Richard Titmuss, one of the founding fathers of the discipline of social policy in the UK, for example, saw the fiscal and occupational arrangements as two other systems of welfare and was anxious to make a case for each (Titmuss 1963; Mann 2009). But there is another way also in which welfare is much bigger than the welfare state. A very high proportion of what we think of as 'welfare' is not the province of the state at all. It is either provided by individuals or collectively generated by families and by informally or formally organised voluntary associations, or purchased in the market (Deakin 1994: xiv–xv).

The book is international in scope. It is informed especially by debates current in international discourse, drawing upon social policy as it is developing within the EU, the Council of Europe, the OECD and the UN. But all exercises have to favour some locations for evidence and argument and that is the case also with this book. The experience in and of the UK is frequently given the front line but the situation in other countries is also considered. Of these, developments in the US are seen to be of singular relevance because so much of what happens there is transported around the world in some form or other. Europe is also, though, an essential reference point, not least because it is the home of a range of political philosophies around welfare. Information for the EU opens up a broad vista and this provides the basis for much of the analysis, especially in the empirically-oriented chapters (5 and 6). Where inter-country comparisons are explicitly made, Germany and Sweden are taken as case study countries along with the UK and the US. The former two countries represent quite different models of welfare to the latter and all four encapsulate key elements of the variation in welfare-related ideology and organisation that is to be found in the highly industrialised world. Regrettably, there is not the space to cover the other parts of the world in detail, although the book is underpinned by the recognition of welfare as part of a universal momentum and struggle.

The book relies for the most part on secondary evidence. In its empirical parts it presents the most up-to-date developments and as much as possible juxtaposes information from different sources and different locations. There are limitations that should be mentioned at the outset, however. Originally, it was intended that the book would focus much more on the 'doing of welfare' than it does. The reasons relate to 'data'. Empirical information on welfare as an aspect of everyday life is limited. The available information is also quite particular – frequently deriving from small-scale and localised research, which is an unreliable base from which to characterise processes at national and international levels. The time period covered by the book also requires a word of explanation. Already a number of references have been made to 'contemporary' in the sense of the period covered. This reference is meant to evoke a set of developments and processes rather than referring rigidly to a particular point in time. To be more specific: this book is located in the period of globalised capitalism and widespread neo-liberalism. This has involved an uncoupling of state and economy and polarisation between an elite and the mass of wage-earners. Corporations are no longer tied to a particular national base nor bound by strict regulation. Capitalism has become 'financialised' and financial capital has become more and more autonomous from what is still called 'the real economy'. Wall Street and the City in London have national addresses but they belong to nowhere. In the last ten years in particular, capitalist finance has become a gigantic gambling casino which trades in currencies, 'securities' and 'derivatives' (Therborn 2009). The neo-liberal policy approach is significant also because it has promoted a policy favouring price stability over employment creation and adopted a critical if not hostile stance towards the welfare state. The book is not a 'post credit crunch' book, in any obvious sense anyway. The crisis, recession actually, is still too recent to allow detailed analysis and hence one risks speculation. But much of the argument here is very pertinent to the recession because it is part of an evolution of the current phase of globalised capitalism rather than a new departure. It is the unfolding of a longer upheaval, part of what Offer (2006: 8) describes as 'a slow shift away from the common welfare and public service as sources of well-being, and towards private benefits'. Hence, the changes which led to the latest recession inform the book throughout.

Structure

The book is structured into three parts. The first part focuses on welfare as a concept and subject of academic work. It consists of two chapters. The aim of the first chapter is to set out the constituent ideas in welfare and the main perspectives through which the concept has been developed. Hence, the classic conceptions of welfare in a number of academic disciplines are reviewed and compared. This chapter also highlights a number of underlying tensions contained in the concept. In the second chapter other concepts take the lead and welfare is in the back seat. The chapter reviews in turn well-being, care, poverty, social exclusion and social capital. The idea is to see what these concepts and approaches reveal about matters relating to welfare and to consider why they have come to eclipse the concept of welfare itself. The insights of both sets of scholarship are compared at the end of the chapter and a broadened conception of welfare is elaborated.

The meaning of welfare is inextricably bound up with on the one hand philosophical ideas and ethical positions and on the other hand policies and political institutions. These are the subject of the next two chapters, comprising the book's second part. Chapter 3 locates welfare in a range of political philosophies, the aim being to provide an outline of the main theoretical frameworks in which political perspectives on welfare are located. Moving on from this, the chapter then considers the main political positions on how collective welfare should be organised and it also explores how these positions are being reformed and updated. Chapter 4 moves on to how welfare is organised as a societal goal. Its lead concept is the welfare state – a form not just of state organisation but of societal organisation. Adopting a comparative approach, this chapter identifies the welfare state's history, pins down its key features (within and across national borders) and charts the main challenges and changes as much of the old welfare settlement comes up for target practice and review.

The third part of the book looks towards the 'doing' and practice of welfare, and is an attempt to explore welfare by looking at some of the contexts in which it is operating. The two chapters here draw extensively on empirical material in order to identify the situation for people in real life and the processes and trajectories associated with different types of organised welfare provision. They consider the search after welfare as a mix of macro- and micro-level activity. The first, chapter 5, takes an overview of material resources, outlining first how people secure welfare in the market and the welfare state. The second part of the chapter examines the broader contours of material resources in society, focusing on how the opportunities available to people are shaped by their resources and background and examining the chances for people to improve their situation. Chapter 6 turns its face in a different direction, looking at welfare as it is a component of family life on the one hand and community and social life on the other. Among the subjects considered in the first part of this chapter are how the family effects distribution and redistribution of income and other resources, and families as a site of care and emotional and other forms of support. The chapter then considers community as a source of welfare. It looks at the contours of civil society engagement and examines evidence on the extent to which people feel integrated into their communities and part of their societies.

A short overview chapter completes the text.

The three parts of the book are separated from each other by an intermezzo section. The purpose here is to direct the focus of the following chapters, in the context of rather broad-ranging discussions which extend beyond the book's allotted space. In each case the intermezzo funnels the discussion to follow from key points of the preceding chapters.

1
Founding Ideas and Approaches

This chapter introduces welfare by outlining its most enduring representations in academic work. As it develops, the chapter tilts towards the historical – the intention is to pinpoint the long-standing concerns that are evoked by welfare and the scholarly approaches through which these have been identified, examined and developed. Following a brief outline of a range of definitions, the second section of the chapter takes us in turn through a discussion of welfare viewed as economic, as a philosophical and political ideal, and as a response to perceived social problems and social ills. In its third part, the chapter engages further with the concept by considering some enduring questions that it raises. These probe the relative *vs* universal nature of welfare, whether it should be thought of in relation to individuals or collectivities, and the matter of whose responsibility it is to provide welfare. We shall see that the concept has a range of meanings and that it is a site of competing accounts and visions.

Origins and Meanings of Welfare

The origins of the term can be traced back at least to the fourteenth century when it meant to fare or journey well (Williams 1976: 281). There is a dual sense of welfare here as both condition and process – captured if we hyphenate the word: wel-fare. Over time, welfare has acquired a diverse set of meanings. Among its many popular references now are material sufficiency, well-being, the absence of negative conditions, physical and mental health, satisfaction of desires, and provision for need within the context of organised services for the needy and the population more broadly.

As mentioned, welfare as a term is not as widely used now as in the past. In the 1970s and 1980s, there were far more publications with 'welfare' in the title as compared with the present period, for instance. There are other indications also that the concept has fallen out of favour. As Dean views it (2006: 21), recent ideological controversy over the nature and purpose of social policies has seen welfare acquire a pejorative connotation. This is true especially in the US, where the term has a powerful negative charge. Its American usage is associated with both safety-net or means-tested benefits and people who depend on them for their income. When this view is unpicked, a connected set of assumptions is revealed. Three such assumptions are noteworthy.

In the first instance, 'welfare' is connected to a moral code that places special value not so much on work as on the work of the poor (Frankel 1966: 151). Adults without an income need to be made to work. This quasi-punitive tradition has deep roots. For example, it was inscribed in the English Poor Law tradition, which dates from the early seventeenth century. This was a regime wherein those who were considered needy through no fault of their own received non-punitive forms of assistance whereas aid to those deemed 'indigent' was organised through regimes of 'correction'. The latter only got help if they subjected themselves to the stringent conditions attached to receiving aid. Their comparators were the 'independent labourers', in many cases the working poor. In effect, assistance to the poor was basically framed in terms of labour supply – aid for the able-bodied should not interfere with the work incentive (ibid.). The term 'welfare to work', so widely used in social policy discourse now, carries these ideas forward, implying a movement from a state of dependency to one of self-sufficiency.

A second set of assumptions connects 'welfare' with the behaviour and assumed character of those who receive public support. As a group these are inscribed with negative characteristics. They are assumed to be if not lazy then lacking a sense of responsibility and 'get up and go'. 'Welfare', then, is a codeword for the presupposition of economic inactivity, dependency on public support, and shiftlessness (Fraser and Gordon 1994a). It is a shorthand for character really – people on 'welfare' lack the necessary moral fibre to be self-supporting. Also embedded in this notion of 'welfare' is a set of beliefs about organised public support. A third set of assumptions homes in on this. While some would hold that organised public systems of aid and support always contain perverse incentives – encouraging 'free riding' (in the sense of people claiming more than their fair share) and lack of independence – a more nuanced version of the argument differentiates between benefits organised around the principles of social insurance and social assistance respectively. A relatively simple division is imposed here, with the former seen to be earned and deserved and the latter acquired through need. When this is applied to individuals, it leads to a division of benefit recipients into two crude categories – those claiming benefits which they are considered to have earned and those receiving monies given on the basis of general need. If labour supply preoccupies the minds of those who plan and design benefit systems, the public imagination tends to be more focused on separating the 'deserving' and the 'undeserving'. This latter preoccupation, too, has deep roots. Historical research in the UK, for example, traces it as far back as the 1860s, dubbing it a 'Victorian idea' (Kidd 2004: 213). Just as one should not see this issue as recent, so also should it not be treated in isolated terms, as if it pertains only to views about those receiving benefits. Rather, the question of who deserves what is fundamental to the fabric of moral and social life (and is the reason why we introduce it so early).

This minimal sense of welfare is, then, an important current in contemporary and historical thought on the subject. As we shall see, though, the pejorative usage of welfare is a rather small part of the universe of the term's usages and origins.

In the academic literature, welfare has been conceptualised very diversely and there is no commonly agreed approach. The following is a sample of definitions, drawing upon different constituent elements and approaches:

the possession of all-purpose means to attain one's ends and/or the satisfaction of one's desires and preferences (Fives 2008: 3–4)

providing some of the conditions for the realisation of mutual security, dignity and respect (Williams 1999: 685)

the common denominator that we all share and which marks us out as members of the same social group (Fitzpatrick 2001: 23)

an overall goal of the political community consisting in the optimal satisfaction of interests which the members of the community have in common (Pusić 1966: 83).

While these writers obviously understand welfare quite differently, viewed in the round the definitions alert us to some foundations of the concept and a broader set of references than we have encountered to date. One set of meanings is of welfare as relative to the group or situation one finds oneself in rather than referring to an absolute set of needs or conditions. Are there core or essential conditions for human welfare? Do we have needs that are universal or are our needs determined by the general conditions and standards of the society in which we live? While Fives (2008) speaks of individual desires and preferences, Williams (1999) sees welfare as realised by mutual security, dignity and respect. This brings us to a second noteworthy reference in the term which is to the collective level and how activity on the part of individuals relates to resources and outcomes for the group or society as a whole and vice versa. This is an issue that runs through most discussions of welfare. Indeed, it is an enduring tension in social provision overall: how is the well-being of particular groups to be set against the situation of the collectivity as a whole? What priority should be given to those in need and how are antagonistic interests to be reconciled? For Fitzpatrick welfare is inherently social – the 'common denominator' that we share by virtue of our social group membership. Fitzpatrick's underlying reference is to 'social welfare', by which is usually meant a collective state of well-being. Finally, there is the question of where the appropriate responsibility for welfare lies. Welfare animates a range of political interests and as the definition by Pusić above suggests politics are

Box 1.1   Three core meanings of welfare in scholarship

Neo-classical Economics	Welfare as preference satisfaction
Political Philosophy/Political Science	Welfare as a political ideal and object of political/state organisation
Social Policy/Social Work/Sociology	Welfare as residing in responses to a range of social problems

shaped fundamentally by responses to welfare-related demands voiced on behalf of different, and usually opposing, constituencies and met in ways that politically favour one sector of society over another. We shall return to these questions again in the final section of the chapter.

It is already obvious that welfare has no fixed meaning. Focusing in on the dominant streams of work helps to make sense of the variation, showing that it is not random but has been historically constructed. Viewed over time, thinking on welfare has developed through three main lines of scholarly activity: as an outcome of markets and economic exchanges, as a philosophical ideal and subject of political contestation and state organisation, as a set of responses to social problems and prevailing social conditions (box 1.1). Each dovetails with the orientations and interests of particular disciplines – although we should not view this too narrowly or in territorial terms.

Welfare in Economistic Thinking

Many perspectives in economics (e.g. Marxism, Keynesianism) have insights to convey about welfare but these have been displaced by what since the 1970s has become the ruling theory – neo-classical economics. In neo-classical (neo-liberal) theory, the endowment of resources, technology and tastes and preferences are taken as given. With their initial endowment of resources, people exchange some of what they have for a combination that will give them more satisfaction. Thus, in this approach the market is given priority as is consumption (choice) over production. The kinds of issue that this scholarship has puzzled over include the nature of welfare as utility (pleasure or satisfaction), the relationship between welfare and an optimum distribution of resources, the matter of individual choice and autonomy, the effectiveness of the market arrangements in achieving welfare, and the priority of welfare in the allocation of public resources (Adiseshiah 1966: 97).

To understand how welfare is conceived within neo-classical economics, we need to have a grasp of utilitarianism, welfarism, and Pareto efficiency. A utilitarian perspective conceives of welfare as the satisfaction of a person's preferences (utilities). In Jeremy Bentham's view, all experiences can be measured on a single scale of pleasure and pain; and pleasure is the only ultimate source of value (Sugden 1993: 1949). A utilitarian approach is primarily focused on welfare as a mental state consequent upon autonomous actions by individuals to satisfy their preferences. Etzioni (1986 as reported in Culyer 1990: 16) identified three main variations in economists' use of the concept of utility. The first is that of pleasure of the self. The second is an expanded version of the first, encompassing the satisfactions achieved through own consumption of goods and those of others. The third usage treats utility as a means of ranking preferences. The underlying theory is that individuals achieve satisfaction from the goods and services that they purchase and this satisfaction is reflected in the prices they are willing to pay for such goods and services. The understanding of welfare, then, is of taste satisfaction associated with exchange and consumption. Gasper (2007: 39) summarises the classic foci and presumptions as a causal chain:

> exogenous preferences and resource endowments →
> income → choice/expenditure → preference fulfilment →
> satisfaction (utility).

He spends therefore he is well!

Welfarism is a related approach, evolving from classical utilitarian theories. Welfarism was developed in a period when it was assumed that the purpose of welfare economics was to produce policy recommendations on how to achieve the social good (Sugden 1993: 1948). Its framework of analysis consists of assigning a numerical index of social welfare to every possible social state (ibid.). To determine how to evaluate a social state it draws on two principles. First, if every individual in society is indifferent between two particular social states, then those states must be assigned the same welfare index. But, and this is the second principle, if at least one individual prefers x to y, and no one prefers y, then x must be assigned a higher value than y. Value is demonstrated by preferences.[1] Welfarism is consequentialist, holding that actions, policies, and/or rules should be evaluated on the basis of their consequences. Welfarist views have been especially influential in law and economics, leading to an approach to policy evaluation that is closely focused on outcomes and measurable achievements (Dean 2010: 103).

The concept of efficiency is another popular criterion for judging welfare in neo-classical economics scholarship. As a judgement on the allocation of goods or income, Pareto efficiency holds that welfare unambiguously increases only if the welfare of any member of society increases and that of no one falls. A society that is making at least one person better off without disimproving anyone's situation is, then, increasing its level of welfare (Fitzpatrick 2001: 13). While it does have the benefit of recognising potential conflict over resources and is in essence a moral position, as a standard of welfare it is almost impossible to fulfil, given that resources are always scarce.

While it might be correct to claim parsimony for the neo-classical economics perspective in that it rests on a small number of assumptions about human beings and their behaviour, such parsimony is not without costs. Individuals' preferences are taken as given and seen as relatively consistent. Nor is there much mystique in human behaviour: people will choose to maximise their satisfactions. That is, people will always act rationally and in their own interests. Utilitarianism certainly does not problematise value as having social components. Indeed, its understanding of social relations is on the primitive side. Society is the aggregate outcome of individual actions, a loose association of individuals connected by contract and consent (Dwyer 2000: 39). Culture, morals, institutions and social processes are just some of the social phenomena rendered devoid of causal sign or significance (Jordan 2008a). Furthermore, willingness to pay has a sacrosanct place in utilitarianism – effective demand is one of the linchpins of the approach. Another is the assumption of the infinite consumer. This, say Drover and Kerans (1993: 6), skews all subsequent debate about welfare since it delegitimises the ethical aspects of questions about redistribution and puts no moral demands on the consumers. All they need to be concerned with is satisfying their preferences. Choice is non-negotiable – people must be free to choose what they want and how to satisfy their preferences. In sum, the ruling theory in economics has a very particular understanding of welfare and leaves unexplored some of the most interesting aspects of the concept.

Welfare in Political Philosophy and Political Science

Political philosophy foregrounds many of these issues. As compared with neo-classical economics, political philosophy and political science have taken a far more reflective approach – they open windows that neo-classical economics keeps firmly shut. Welfare fits well as a concern here for it is seen to be inextricably bound up with moral precepts and discussions relating to equality, justice, freedom and rights, and how welfare as a goal of political life can be realised in public institutions and practice. Each of these streams of scholarship – the philosophical and the political – merits discussion, even if space constraints ordain brevity.

A quick route into the complex philosophical issues is through the (admittedly oversimplified) divide between liberals and egalitarians. They differ on many matters including the nature of private property rights, justifications for and implications of welfare as a focus of activity on the part of the state, the constitution of justice and equality in their own

right and in regard to resource distribution, and the obligations and conditions that make for membership of the political community. The very meaning of welfare is at stake. In
the liberal or individualist orientation, welfare is lodged in
individual autonomy and satisfaction of desires (reminiscent
of utilitarianism). Human relations are seen in competitive
terms – all against all – and when people manage to co-
operate it is mainly out of self-interest. In contrast, egalitarians argue for collective provision and justify it on numerous
grounds. One rationale is to protect the vulnerable (for
example, children and elderly people, the poor or people who
cannot provide for themselves). A second is to compensate
for and ameliorate inequalities. But there is also a broader
argument about collective welfare, larger than the interests
or needs of any one group. State action has a vital role in this
perspective: 'Welfare benefits are outward and visible signs
of the desire of the majority to help their less fortunate fellow
men and in this sense are concerned with developing a sense
of community and involvement of one person with another'
(Plant et al. 1980: 56). The institutions and processes associated with the welfare state in particular are seen to serve a
socially integrative function – they advance equality and help
to mobilise a society of intimate communal bonds (Tawney
1931; Titmuss 1974). The liberal and egalitarian positions
(along with others) will be outlined further below and
explored more fully in chapter 3.

With the foregoing discussion we have already entered
the territory of the second relevant seam of work around
welfare: the nature, extent and legitimate role of the state.
Citizenship is useful as a guiding frame here. It is a way of
both thinking about and actually organising what people are
entitled to by virtue of being citizens of their country (B.
Turner 1993; Isin and Wood 1999; Lister 2004). Understood
especially in the sense of national community – the entitlements and responsibilities assigned to being 'British', 'American', 'Swedish' and so forth – it gives effect to the meaning
of 'community'. Variations in citizenship and the rights available to both citizens and non-citizens spell out the extent to
which there exists a common set of institutions, categories
and services designed for all (Fraser and Gordon 1994b: 90).
The classic work here is that of T. H. Marshall (1950), who

spoke of three types of citizen rights – civil (which guarantee people basic freedoms), political (which give them rights to participate in political processes), and social (which confer rights to a range of social services and income supports). For Marshall, whose societal template was England, these rights were developed sequentially as part of a modernisation process, with social rights as the triumph of politics over markets (and hence the vanquishing of inequalities based on social class). The latter is a form of equal recognition of each person regardless of their origins or condition. Marshall's account was incomplete, though – what he failed to point out was that citizenship in England and elsewhere was based initially on political citizenship for male property owners and that citizenship was only gradually extended to men from all classes and then later still to women (Woodward and Kohli 2001: 5).

As a descriptive framework, Marshall's threefold conception of rights holds relatively well, though. It maps, loosely, onto the two philosophical traditions mentioned in the last paragraph. The liberal perspective construes citizenship in terms of the protection of individual status and freedom of action – it is that which is necessary to ensure that people are protected against the constraints and harms caused by the behaviour of others. This view favours a limited conception of rights, focused on the first two of Marshall's rights' categories: civil and political rights. The second approach – the civic republican perspective – emphasises participation in the community and public life. In this view life is a collaboration between vulnerable but co-operative beings (Dean 2008: 58). Citizenship, therefore, is a form of pooling of individual sovereignty so as to promote social order and collective well-being (ibid.). This view is very much in favour of social rights, seeing them as necessary for a fully-functioning state and society. As a shorthand to grasp the difference between the two positions, it is helpful to note that the liberal perspective stands the individual out from the group or community whereas in the republican approach the needs and interests of the group or collectivity as a whole are to the fore.

The model of citizenship that prevails in a country or is argued for is closely related to the type of welfare state that exists or is sought. The term 'welfare state', which is the subject of chapter 4, connotes a particular form of the state, one oriented to meeting needs and addressing a range of welfare-related exigencies. In this state form, government takes responsibility for those unable to provide for their own welfare and, depending on how widely the notion of public welfare (or social citizenship) extends, guarantees not just support but security in a range of eventualities. The welfare state constitutes, therefore, a very different approach to the Poor Law, with its focus on meeting the worst cases of need only and its tests of deservingness. Marshall's (1950) three-fold classification of citizenship captures much about the welfare state and its variations: the more expansive are social rights the more developed is the welfare state. Political science treats the welfare state as a structure of power especially, both an outcome of political processes and in turn effecting political intervention. It does not just happen therefore but, as we shall see, is fought for and remains contested.

The Social Meanings of Welfare

The idea of social welfare provides a further counterpoint again to those depictions of welfare discussed to date. As developed in the disciplines of Social Policy[2] and social work, and sociology to a lesser extent, considerations of social welfare are more complex than could be imagined from a neo-classical economics perspective. If economists work with preferences as a proxy for welfare, social scientists tend to focus on needs and social problems and responses to both. The concept of need is seen to describe something about human nature that is more essential than the economists' 'preferences' (Fitzpatrick 2001: 7). It is also a less individualistic concept. Welfare in a social vein is intimately connected, then, with societal ends and functioning, especially in terms of the measures to be taken to address such phenomena as poverty, unemployment, ill-health, social inequality. The social disciplines share considerable common ground with philosophy and political science. Indeed, many of the debates in political philosophy were also rehearsed from a social perspective. But they tended to be fractured through three lenses:

- views about the nature of the human condition and how it can be improved;
- investigations of the nature and origins of social problems and how they are connected to social organisation and the (mal)distribution of resources;
- convictions about the implications and effectiveness of different approaches to social intervention and reform and how they sit with prevailing norms and ideologies.

In the early days especially, social criticism – of prevailing conditions and the functioning of different forms of policy and collective response in light of need – was central. This early work 'fixed' welfare in a particular frame: social problem solving.[3] Three ideas capture the early development of the thinking about welfare in the social disciplines: poverty/need, the moral make-up of the poor, social reform and appropriate provision.

In a historical context, social investigators and moral activists were key welfare agents. The nineteenth- and early twentieth-century social reform tradition, as in Britain (England especially) and the US, was committed to gathering factual information and utilising it to point the way to appropriate organisational and moral principles for social action and social institutions. The treatment of poverty, in particular, is revealing of both the early analyses of social welfare and ways of thinking about it that have endured. There was a rush to poverty studies in England in the late nineteenth and early twentieth centuries (and in the US too, only somewhat later (O'Connor 2001)).[4] These had two originating sets of interests. On the one hand, empirically studying poverty satisfied a genuine interest on the part of reformers and others in the circumstances in which certain sectors of the population were living and the conditions and causes of deprivation. There was a sense of trying to determine basic needs and the conditions of subsistence, to find poverty's objective core and also to see how it was a product of social and economic conditions (Hewitt 1998). Social investigation was motivated especially by a conviction that gaining empirical knowledge about a 'problem' is an important step towards solving it. The belief in so-called scientific methods of investigation led to a hunger for 'facts'. Research and reform were closely linked. Or, and this brings us to the second motivating interest: the 'facts' suggested that poverty was at least in part due to the behaviour and predispositions of the poor. The poor rather than their poverty were a prominent motivator of poverty research, and have remained so (especially in the US). At root here is the matter of the moral significance of the poor and the phenomenon of pauperism. This is something that has troubled politicians, social commentators and theologians from the Middle Ages (Glennerster 2004: 15).

This brings us to the third preoccupation of early poverty research: social provision. By the turn of the twentieth century in Britain (somewhat later again in the US), the social reform ideology was permeated by a desire to provide decent treatment and social incentives for the 'respectable' and to separate them from the 'residuum' (Hay 1975). Institutions of welfare (social services provided on a statutory and/or voluntary basis, for example) become important in this context. The historical origins and early development of both the disciplines of Social Policy and social work predisposed them to the transformative power of intervention (first charitable and later bureaucratic and professional), and gave them a particular interest in how well different types of intervention functioned in response to social problems and social needs.[5] One of the most widespread historical references to welfare as social, then, was to the services and arrangements that should be put in place to effect intervention for the relief of poverty, deprivation and need. Early welfare thinking (and poverty research also) helped to lay out the conditions that should attach to the distribution of public resources to those considered needy. In Britain and the US especially, it left a sense of deep concern about state-organised welfare as a response to poverty and need. Tests of need and other demonstrations of worthiness are among the legacies bequeathed by this concern. Welfare was in many ways taken for granted in this scholarship – in a climate where reflexivity about the normative basis of scholarship was rare, welfare was self-evidently a good thing. Social progress could be achieved provided change was managed

Box 1.2 Focus of classic scholarship on welfare

Neo-classical Economics	Individuals' resource endowments, exchanges in markets and their impact on preference satisfaction
Political Philosophy/Political Science	Values, ethics, political ideals, citizenship, the welfare state
Social Policy/Social Work/Sociology	Need, poverty and deprivation, social conditions, different forms of social response to need and social problems

in the right way. The treasure at the rainbow's end was the optimum response to welfare conceived as individual need and social problems.

In sum, what one might call the classic streams of work on welfare emphasised the economic, philosophical/political and some social aspects (box 1.2). Viewed together like this, they have an extensive reach. They make reference, for example, to the community, the market, the state and to welfare as having economic, political and social dimensions. They also point to the limits of a discipline-specific approach. The big questions actually run across disciplines. Taking a broader view allows us to set out some over-arching issues (and releases us from the straightjacket imposed by disciplinary boundaries).

Overarching Questions about Welfare

Looking across the deliberations on welfare, there are three sets of what might be called strong questions or dilemmas (box 1.3). Although they have been touched on already, they merit some discussion because much of the thinking and research on welfare reflects efforts to grapple with these difficult issues.

> **Box 1.3   Enduring questions and tensions in welfare scholarship**
>
> | Focus | Key questions |
> | --- | --- |
> | Welfare as relative or universal | To what extent does welfare vary by context or situation or are there universal human needs? |
> | Welfare as individual or collective | Is the idea of social welfare meaningful and under what conditions is it possible? |
> | The appropriate provider of welfare | To what degree is welfare appropriately provided by the state, family, community, market? |

The Relative or Universal Nature of Welfare

A first vexing issue centres on the question of whether welfare is relative or universal. A relative understanding seems justified in light of the variation in the meaning given to welfare across time period, culture and society. Pusić (1966: 82) takes the relativism of welfare to an extreme in suggesting that welfare is an 'empty' concept in that its meaning is determined by contingencies of place and time. A relativistic view also pervades the utilitarian approach: welfare is the achievement of that which individuals desire or want. Much of the absolute as against relative view of welfare crystallises around the nature of need, something that has proved very controversial.[6]

One influential strand of work sought to identify a set of universal needs. A needs-based approach cuts across many of the more difficult philosophical questions by positing a universal and objective set of needs. If such a universal set of needs exists, then it can form the basis for the non-market allocation of resources (Drover and Kerans 1993: 4). Need is a totally different approach to that of preference or even want. Abraham Maslow (1970) did seminal work on need, drawing up a hierarchical model of human needs, based on five different kinds of need. These are in descending order of importance: physiological (air, water, sleep), safety (home and family), belonging (social connectedness), esteem (self-esteem, confidence, respect of others) and self-actualisation (morality, creativity, problem solving). Maslow's work implies that only when physiological needs are satisfied should we think of meeting safety needs, and so forth. There are other conceptions of need which are neither hierarchical nor asocial, however. Doyal and Gough (1991), working with insights from sociology, psychology and political science, sought to draw up an ethical theory of need that takes full account of people's embeddedness in social life. For them a basic need refers to the objective preconditions required for a person to attain a goal; if such preconditions are not in place, then harm will ensue. Their social orientation is reflected in their conclusion that there are two universal needs: avoiding serious harm, ability to participate as an effective member of society. These needs, they claim, have an objective core. Prerequisites for their fulfilment are, respectively, mental and physical health and autonomy of agency (in the sense of people being able to make informed choices). These two needs are in turn dependent on the satisfaction of a range of prerequisites, factors which according to Doyal and Gough everywhere contribute to improved health and autonomy. As set out in box 1.4, these are for health – nutritious food and clean water, protective housing, non-hazardous work and physical environments, safe birth control and childbearing, and appropriate health care. Autonomy requires security in childhood, significant primary relationships, physical security, economic security, and appropriate education. Doyal and Gough stress that these are socially relative and so may vary in importance and impact within and across societies.

Even if one could agree on a basic list (and there are notable omissions from the list in box 1.4, such as mental health), there are major problems with the approach. Of these I draw attention to two. First, there is an individualistic bias in it, especially in the sense of not recognising how much our self-realisation is dependent on the recognition and respect we receive from others. Feminist and other theorists have been critical of this, pointing out that assumptions of autonomy are based on a reading of male behaviour in western

---

Box 1.4   Doyal and Gough's basic and intermediate needs

Health

adequate nutritious food and clean water;
adequate protective housing;
non-hazardous work and physical environments;
safe birth control and childbearing;
appropriate health care.

Autonomy

significant primary relationships;
security in childhood;
physical security;
economic security;
appropriate education.

---

societies and that human development is defined by a process of connection to others rather than disconnection (Gilligan 1982; Drover and Kerans 1993). Relationships are therefore central. On the basis of this position, some have developed an argument that receiving recognition (of our own needs and our individuality and the needs of oppressed minorities) is fundamental to justice (Fraser 2001, 2003; Fraser and Honneth 2003; Honneth 2004; Young 2008). Politics is, therefore, a struggle not just for resources but for identity and recognition too.

Secondly, needs are relative in other respects also. Quite a large literature suggests that needs are interpreted – that far from a need being objective or self-evident, there is a process of 'need interpretation' which is lodged in social and political discourse and decision making. What is accepted as a need is, therefore, that which has been legitimated. An underlying reference here is to the twin processes whereby needs are turned into claims (by individuals, groups, sectors of society and so forth) and claims are adjudicated on (Fraser 1989; Dean 2010). Rather than signifying an objective reality, needs are to be understood in terms of how they are labelled and constructed by different groups in specific contexts and the responses to such 'constructions' (Lister 2010: 181). This way of thinking problematises the processes involved in the articulation and interpretation of needs rather than a list of needs. Bradshaw's (1972) taxonomy of needs conveys the idea well. He distinguishes between normative needs (needs determined by experts), felt needs (needs that people themselves identify when asked), expressed needs (those articulated) and comparative needs (the shortfall or deficiency experienced by one group vis-à-vis another or the population at large). This serves to convey the idea that there is nothing essential in need. A second relevant point that comes out of this scholarship is the claim that the welfare state is centrally engaged in a process of 'need interpretation' (Fraser 1989). Whether through the procedures of actually adjudicating on claims from different individuals and groups or the way in which different situations are recognised as meriting support or not, or indeed at a more abstract level in terms of representations of different groups and situations, the welfare state is one of the major sites within which needs are interpreted. Engaged in a micro-politics of power, it is, therefore, part of a system of 'power–knowledge' (along the lines suggested by the perspective of Michel Foucault (1991)). This kind of perspective certainly debunks the idea of the welfare state as a straightforward response to social problems. It also implies the importance of having a 'voice' or say, of being heard, and suggests that some people or sectors of society need the resources to mobilise around their claims.[7]

Overall, the relative *vs* absolute nature of basic needs continues as an unresolved tension in the literature and also in policy debate.

The Individual or Collective Nature of Welfare

A second enduring question is about whether welfare can be thought of meaningfully in collective terms. There are different ways of framing this. Glennerster (1989: 114) puts it in terms of what is the appropriate scope for social as distinct from individual action. One could see it also as being about whether there is such an entity as community or society when it comes to questions of welfare. The individualist or liberal strain in scholarship is strong and has been especially prominent for the last three to four decades. This questions the very notion of a 'general or social welfare'. For classical liberalism only persons are capable of experiencing welfare. Welfare and distributive justice are, therefore, treated as strictly separate (Barry 1990: 18). Welfare in this view has strong overtones of self-sufficiency. This is, as Heclo (1986: 182) notes, a supremely individualistic position, focusing on the capacity of the person to go his or her own way, to enjoy the fruits of his or her labour, to be unbeholden and unentangled. There is no welfare function for society as a whole in this view.

To posit that there is such a thing as collective welfare is to maintain that welfare is more than the sum of individual welfares. It is, in effect, to see welfare as having social constituents. There are two underlying claims. First, that mutual dependence, as against independence, defines the human condition (we shall discuss this in more detail in the next chapter). Secondly, that there are social values, purposes and goods that ought to be promoted independently of individual choice. The existence of a 'we' and an 'our' is not in doubt; rather what is contested is who constitutes the 'we' and what obligations or responsibilities members of particular groups have to fellow members and to 'others'.

This raises the matter of justice in general and social justice in particular. Positions on this vary also. At one end are classical liberals for whom justice is not a prime consideration – the market cannot be the author of injustice because the market does not act with intent. For Hayek (1976) one of the high priests of neo-liberalism, for example, social justice has no substantive existence – it is a mirage – because in a free society based on the market inequalities arise naturally as a result of circumstances over which no one has any control. The state cannot provide redress for such inequalities, not least because to do so governments require knowledge of individual preferences, a knowledge that they cannot legitimately acquire without fatal interference in the functioning of a free market. Moreover, in a pluralistic society the state should be neutral between the various conceptions of the good that are on offer to its citizens as there are no agreed criteria of justice (Gray 1983). For egalitarians, on the other hand, justice and equality are inextricably related and greater fairness involves a diminution of inequalities (Weale 1978: 3). Egalitarians work hard to elaborate justice as a social concept, rather than one pertaining to relations among individuals. For Frankena (1962), for example, justice connotes the notion of a good-working society and has within it also some idea about an allotment of something to persons. Justice is, therefore, the result of deliberate actions, not simply a matter of how things come about but how we respond to them.

All of this is closely related to the third major tension: whose responsibility is it to provide welfare?

Who is the Appropriate Provider?

This question is in essence about agency in the field of welfare. While it may be taken for granted in today's western societal model, the state has never been the only significant actor in the field. Harris (2009: 5) points out that for much of the nineteenth century social responsibilities in Britain (and, one might add, elsewhere) were largely matters of civic, voluntary or associational ties and that it was only as the twentieth century advanced that 'social evils' and responsibility for dealing with them came to be identified as 'national' and hence an appropriate sphere of activity for the state. Looked at historically and even still today, there is a quadrangle of agents involved in providing welfare: the state, religious bodies in a variety of forms, what might be called mutual aid or self-help, and the market (Deakin et al. 2004). The interplay between these actors in the field of welfare has taken different shapes at different times and given rise to a variety of social, economic and political forms.

Over time, the state has moved from a marginal role in welfare to a central one. Sometimes this was for reasons of efficiency and effectiveness – the scale of the need being such as to call forth a great response. Or, the growth of a role for the state in welfare may have had political origins – Chancellor Bismarck instituted social insurance in late nineteenth-century Germany, for example, mainly in the interests of binding the loyalty of workers to the newly unified German state. In addition, some political perspectives call for a state that is active in welfare – the egalitarian position outlined earlier, for example, requires large-scale state action to ensure wide access to resources and opportunities. The prevailing notion of citizenship is also an important determinant of the role and extent of the state in welfare provision. From a welfare perspective, citizenship may imply state provision of a minimal set of entitlements – the avoidance of hunger and destitution – or the meeting of all welfare-related needs.

But there have always been alternative providers of welfare. Historically, the charitable endeavours of religious institutions of all kinds were foundational to collective welfare. The religious communities played a major role in many countries, raising funds for relief of the 'less fortunate' and expending resources on the creation and maintenance of welfare-related institutions. As a provider of alms, the church was in some countries the first and in many cases the only recourse for those in need (Deakin et al. 2004). In Ireland, for example, the religious institutions set up the first hospitals and schools. While the western development trajectory has seen the state take over much of the role of service provider, some churches continue to offer a community and social infrastructure for their members. Moreover, patterns of migration and political development in many parts of the world have made for an increased role for churches and religious communities in the welfare of their members.

Thirdly, there is individual and collective self-help. The family or wider kin group is the original welfare unit with norms about family obligation foundational to most cultures. Outside of the family, the most important manifestations of collective mutual aid historically were various forms of community organisation, either self-help on the part of the working-class sections of society or charity on the part of the upper classes. There were many institutions set up by the working class to protect their own interests and resist the negative tendencies of charity and patronage on the part of the wealthy. These included, as well as trade unions, so-called friendly societies, co-operatives and mutual agencies. In addition to organised community activity, there has always been informal mutual aid: 'the kindness of the poor to one another' (Deakin et al. 2004: 3). These various kinds of community-based activity have coalesced into what we now think of as 'civil society': extensive networks of voluntary bodies, charities, non-governmental organisations (NGOs), and communal associations of various kinds that occupy a gap between the state and the market (ibid.).

Finally, the market is another important locus of welfare. Its role in preference satisfaction, wealth creation and income distribution is especially significant from a welfare perspective because it gives people (theoretically anyway) the income to provide for their own welfare. Much of the debate that is going on today about the welfare state seeks an increased role for the market in welfare provision. This is not just about people being self-sufficient and securing their own income through employment. It is also about service provision – the state is either being downgraded as a direct welfare service provider or is seeking 'partners' in the endeavour. The market also plays an indirect role in welfare through providing the means for philanthropy (Deakin et al. 2004). In the US for example, charitable giving is widely promoted and receives official sanction and support in the many tax reliefs allowed for such giving. In 2009 charitable giving in the US is estimated to have amounted to over $300 billion.[8]

There are two important points to retain here. First, the provision of and for welfare is not the preserve of any single actor or agent – it is, therefore, better seen as part of a system. Second, that system is intimately connected with a range of ideas about what the need is, what is the appropriate response, and whose role it is to provide for those who cannot secure their own welfare and for those aspects of welfare that transcend individual well-being.

Overview

Taking an overview, there are a number of notable points about welfare in classic scholarship. First, there are competing accounts of what constitutes welfare and how it is attained. In a range of classical work, welfare has been thought of in terms of three alternative sets of ideas: economic exchanges, a philosophical ideal and form of political organisation, and a response to social problems and social ills. A second striking point is how the different approaches have tended to proceed along their own tracks (see box 1.2 above). The neo-classical economics perspective views welfare primarily in material terms and identifies the main sources and determinants of welfare as generated by market exchanges or through the provision of a limited range of public goods. This is the least equivocal of the three approaches considered. It is also the one that most clearly states what welfare is. The philosophical/political and social perspectives tend to think more in terms of 'welfare as' rather than 'welfare is'. In this and other ways they recognise welfare as normative and contested and as contingent on context. Viewed through a political/philosophical lens, welfare is situated within a range of beliefs about the appropriate moral order in society and the appropriate distribution of resources. Welfare is, then, reflected in political organisation, political contestation and different conceptions of the role of the state. The social approaches locate welfare, often loosely conceived, in the need for and achievement of organised forms of social support and intervention particularly in response to perceived needs and 'social problems'. Their interest in welfare directs them especially (but not by any means exclusively) to a subsection of the population – those who cannot provide for themselves, the 'needy' sectors of society.

The differences between the perspectives are not just differences of a descriptive order but involve very different ways of seeing and understanding human behaviour. The standard economics textbook variant sees welfare in terms of money, material resources, market-based voluntary exchanges and rational behaviours of individuals; the politico-philosophical position sees welfare as shaping and shaped by normative and political questions and settlements around access to resources and the distribution of relative power and authority; social welfare connotes a societal arrangement which takes into account the well-being of all but especially the poorer sections of the population.

Thirdly, there are of course overlaps and these are as useful for the present enterprise as pointing out differences. The approaches share an interest in the functioning of key institutions. Furthermore, they draw attention to a diversity of types of agency: the marketised individual, the politically conscious and active individual or group, and agency oriented towards responding to the vulnerable and social needs more broadly. Hence, the classical variants of welfare lend it powerful resonances, not least a critical approach to the role of the state and a discourse about a range of societal and political institutions and concerns about people's material situation and objective circumstances.

2
Well-being and Other Challenges to Conventional Understandings of Welfare

There are a number of gaps in the theorisations of welfare considered thus far. Agency, especially in the sense of people making choices and acting on them, has hardly figured. One consequence is that the original meaning of welfare as doing and faring well has not been brought out. The perspectives reviewed are poor also at accounting for how economic and other actions are embedded in social relations and how welfare is the outcome of broad-based social action rather than a response to social problems. It is telling also that up to now we have hardly encountered the family, with its characteristic structure of assistance and assumptions of obligation and support. Furthermore, welfare theory, especially in its economic and political variants, lacks a conception of the actualities of real lives. A more rounded understanding of welfare is necessary and that, in a nutshell, is the guiding interest of this chapter.

An explosion of new work in the last decades helps to round out conceptions of welfare. Terms such as well-being, quality of life, happiness, life satisfaction, social exclusion, capabilities, social capital have lit up the field. In this chapter we pick up and elaborate on a number of relevant movements in thinking and research which are proving influential. These movements are lodged in four relevant sets of developments. The first is the move to subjective well-being. This opens up the idea that welfare might be broader than heretofore conceived, not least in that how people feel about their life and situation is, arguably, as important as the conditions in which they consume and live. Secondly, the foregrounding of agency, resources and choice by concepts like well-being and Amartya Sen's capabilities suggests that how people react to their situation and the freedoms that they can exercise are key elements in their welfare. Thirdly, there is the matter of how people's personal relationships and their disposition towards others are implicated in and contribute to welfare. Fourthly, we consider work that locates welfare in societal processes and identifies how such processes generate or deplete social and other forms of resources. While in none of these is welfare the leading concept, they each yield powerful insights.

In some ways, the developments reflect the relative hegemony of particular disciplines or fields. As long as neo-classical economics dominated, for example, concepts derived from the measurement of market transactions – such as GDP – were to the fore in research on welfare (Gasper 2007: 23). But as the more social disciplines interested themselves in welfare and related concepts, the approach changed and the driving set of interests became more diverse. In general, the story is of different interests feeding off each other and overlapping in key emphases and concerns. However, because the relevant literatures have often developed separately, this chapter requires us to engage in some creative juxtaposition – to make linkages across scholarship that has often proceeded along parallel tracks. Similar perspectives and ideas sometimes achieve prominence in separate fields. It should be pointed out in advance that the objective is not to treat the different concepts in detail – that would be impossible within the space available – but rather to mine their insights for how welfare is or might be conceived.

The Rise and Rise of Well-being

While a traditional recourse in conceptualising welfare was to income and access to material goods, people's evaluations of their personal situation and mental orientation are now very popular. The growth of positive psychology has been instrumental in this. This school turns attention to positive mental states, shifting the focus from dysfunction to function and moving from a problems focus (as epitomised by work on poverty, for example) to identify the extent to which people could be said to be happy and flourishing. This work applauds the successful, thriving individual or community. The accent is placed on positive experiences (well-being, optimism, happiness) and character strengths (the capacity for love, social connectedness, originality) (Haworth and Hart 2007: 2). It has succeeded in transforming the entire field.

There are two main conceptual approaches to subjective well-being – the Benthamite subjective-hedonic individualistic perspective and the Aristotelian objective-eudaimonic relational approach (Bruni and Porta 2005: 20).

The hedonic tradition emphasises the integrity of people's own judgements and personal freedom (Phillips 2006: 32). Some of its elements will be familiar from the discussion of utilitarianism in the last chapter. Consumption and pleasure are keywords. By definition concerned with the attainment of pleasure and the avoidance of negative emotion or pain, the focus of hedonic psychological research is 'the happy person'. We are familiar with this from the popular media. TV shows, for example that of Oprah Winfrey, have been popularising the constituent ideas for quite a while now. The assessment of people's subjective well-being typically ranges over three components: life satisfaction, presence of positive mood, and the absence of negative mood (Diener 1984; Diener and Lucas 1999). This kind of work taps into people's emotional state and aspects of their psychological well-being such as feeling satisfied, being healthy, showing an interest in other people, having a sense of life achievement, and being in control (Hills and Argyle 2002; Searle 2008).

As part of the growth of hedonic perspectives (but not limited to it), happiness has come to the fore as a leading concept in the field. In fact, happiness research is claimed by some to be fast becoming a 'new science'.[1] In this perspective, levels of individual happiness or emotional state are taken as a key indicator of quality of life and well-being. The usual research method is to ascertain people's self-assessments of their emotional state in a number of pre-determined domains or dimensions. A spur to much research into happiness and subjective well-being was the economist Easterlin's (1974) research showing that the average happiness levels reported by Americans had not risen for decades despite a doubling in average incomes. The 'Easterlin paradox' as it became known suggested that economic and social advancement were becoming uncoupled (Searle 2008) and raised doubts about the priority that should be given to economic growth as a policy objective. Why should we pursue economic growth if it fails to make people any happier? This has led to calls to make happiness the avowed goal of policy (Layard 2005). The Kingdom of Bhutan is a world leader in this, having made a formal commitment to happiness as a national objective (box 2.1).

An alternative exposition of well-being is the eudaimonic relational conceptualisation. Eudaimonic approaches are concerned with positive functioning; well-being rather than happiness is their leading concept. The ideal is the life well lived in the sense of individuals fulfilling their potential and involving themselves in pursuits that have value and meaning for them. Such theorists distinguish well-being from happiness by arguing that not all desires and pleasures contribute

---

Box 2.1 Gross National Happiness in Bhutan

The term Gross National Happiness (GNH) was coined in 1972 by Bhutan's former King Jigme Singye Wangchuck. He used the phrase to signal his commitment to building an economy that would serve Bhutan's unique culture based on Buddhist spiritual values. The concept serves as a unifying vision for Bhutan's planning process. Proposed policies in Bhutan are GNH proofed, an assessment similar in nature to the environmental impact and other tests which are increasingly required in Europe, the US and elsewhere. The four pillars of GNH are the promotion of sustainable development, preservation and promotion of cultural values, conservation of the natural environment, and establishment of good governance.

Source: http://www.grossnationalhappiness.com

to well-being and some may even cause harm. Popular resonances here would include personal growth and self-development. Drawing on the work of Aristotle (384–22 BC), the eudaimonic understanding of well-being takes its lead from the concept of 'human flourishing' and the idea of realising one's true self or 'daimon' through the actualisation of one's potential (Ryan and Deci 2001). As Gasper (2007: 26) describes it, the Aristotelian tradition understands well-being to mean well-living. The latter is the more active term and does not, in economics anyway, carry any utilitarian assumptions. In contrast to the utilitarian view of man as a pleasure-maximising agent, it sees well-being as the fulfilment of our deeper nature and incorporates the idea that well-being means having a sense of purpose in life: 'participation in civic life, having friends, loving and being loved' (Bruni and Porta 2005: 8).

Just as with happiness, research effort is devoted to identifying people's psychological needs and the conditions associated with meeting them. The focus is not how happy people feel, though, but how well they feel they are fulfilling their goals. Eudaimonic well-being tends to be measured by questions about autonomy, self-determination, interest and engagement, aspirations and motivation, and determining whether people have a sense of meaning, direction or purpose in life. The approach of Ryff (1989) is a good example (box 2.2).

The turn to subjective well-being provides a welcome corrective to the classic understandings in several respects. For example, it shifts the focus away from what people buy and consume to their feelings and subjective responses to their situation. Moreover, it resists taking income or other aspects of people's 'external' lives as proxies for their well-being and is inclusive of life spheres beyond the market. Above all, though, the approach valorises people's assessments of their situation, challenging the tendency for researchers and other experts to 'know' without consulting people. The move to subjective well-being has been said to represent a shift from negative outsider categories which dissect people's lives according to areas of professional specialisation and towards research approaches which are participatory and person-centred (White and Ellison 2007: 159). The subjective well-

---

Box 2.2   Dimensions of psychological well-being

Self-acceptance (feeling good about yourself while aware of your limitations)
Positive relations with others
Environmental mastery (shaping the environment so as to meet personal needs and desires)
Autonomy (self-determination and personal authority)
Purpose in life
Personal growth (making the best of talents and capacities)

Source: Ryff 1989

---

being approach also is sympathetic to valuing more qualitative features of life. That said, the focus on subjective well-being has certain weaknesses. The happiness approach, in particular, runs the risk of prioritising short-term, pleasure-seeking activity and is relatively insensitive to the context in which the emotion is experienced (Wilkinson 2007). Misgivings have also been expressed about the individualistic orientation and the assumption that our behaviour is guided by our own pleasure or sense of fulfilment. In a sense at root here, again, is the individual–collective question – does pleasure and well-being emanate from ourselves or from those around us?

Broadening Well-being in the Direction of Agency and Resources

The concept of well-being has a more general application also as a description of the state of individuals' life situation or 'being' (McGillivray 2007; Veenhoven 2007). Here it shades into an approach which links people's subjective well-being with their objective circumstances. The interest in connecting people's assessment of their mental state with the resources and experiences that they have available has led to an extensive literature across a range of disciplines (Searle 2008). This dual focus is part of the appeal of the concept of well-being. Another perceived strength is the concept's sense of multi-dimensionality – it typically incorporates physical well-being, material well-being, social well-being, and psychological well-being (Felce and Perry 1995). In essence, work on a more general concept of well-being is pushing the concept towards agency and a greater recognition of people's embeddedness in relations and contexts. There are a number of strands.

One is work on quality of life. This interests itself especially in the physical and (increasingly) social conditions in which people live and the links to illness on the one hand and satisfaction with life on the other.[2] It has a strong interest in functioning, whether conceived to refer to mental and physical health or more broadly in terms of the range of relationships and activities that people are involved in and how engaged they are in such relationships. Health is probably the leading domain, though. There are hundreds of health-related quality of life measures and the term has even got its own acronym – HQROL. The World Health Organisation has played a leading role in promoting health as a vital aspect of quality of life. It has defined health not just as absence of illness but 'as a state of complete physical, mental and social well-being' (cited in Phillips 2006: 40). In general nowadays, both physical and mental functioning are to the fore in conceptions of well-being from a health perspective (e.g. Kawachi and Berkman 2000).

A second and arguably the most influential conceptualisation of well-being is that which follows from the work of the economist Amartya Sen (1984, 1992, 1999, *inter alia*). His is a normative theory which is based around the question of what makes a good life for human beings. He concludes that it is their capabilities – the freedom they have to do what they want to and be who they want to be. Sen's interest in capabilities grew out of dissatisfaction with the straightjacket of welfare economics and its conviction that the measure of a good society is the extent to which pleasure is maximised. For him well-being is to be assessed in terms of people's capability to engage in valuable activities or acts and to reach valuable states of being, functionings. It is not resources or command over commodities per se that matter in determining quality of life or even justice. Rather, Sen suggests a change of paradigm: from commodities to capabilities or from goods to what they allow people to obtain and do. Opportunities are more important for him than resources or goods (which are means rather than ends). There is a strong message in Sen's work for the aims of public policy: instead of redistribution of income and goods it should concern itself with nurturing capabilities and it should desist from treating people as objects and instead consider them as subjects and actors (De Leonardis 1993: 187).

His perspective invests hugely in agency but also has a sense of state or condition – the former relates to 'doings' and the latter to 'beings'. Both doing and being are connected in the concept of 'functionings' (the illustrative examples of which include healthfulness, longevity, literacy). The critical element, though, is capabilities. It is these that confer the freedom or opportunity to achieve certain preferred lifestyles. People (should) have capability sets – resources to achieve whatever it is they value. This is close to what is known as positive freedom or 'freedom for'. Our well-being in Sen's view, then, is determined both by our set of capabilities and our set of functionings. Sen adopts an expansive conception of what is valuable in human life, rather than specifying desired outcomes. He therefore does not subscribe to the view of universal basic needs. He has, though, focused attention on what he calls 'basic capabilities' (escaping morbidity and mortality, for example), although he has never provided an indication of a range of appropriate functionings or capabilities.[3] Among other things, this makes the concept of capabilities difficult to operationalise and interpret. In policy-making circles for example, it has often been interpreted as human capital rather than human capabilities (Dean 2010: 84).

Sen's work has been very influential. Key elements of his approach are reflected in the UN's approach to human development, which encompasses both meeting basic needs and extending capabilities. In place since the 1990s, this has the goal of 'putting people back at the center of the development process in terms of economic debate, policy and advocacy'. The associated series of reports and data sets attempt to foreground conditions of life in the context of the links between human well-being and economic development and to measure progress against benchmarks or goals set by the international community. The Human Development Index (HDI) is key in this context (box 2.3).[4] It is a composite statistic used to rank countries by level of 'human development' and to separate developed (high development), developing (middle development), and underdeveloped (low development) countries. It is computed on the basis given in box 2.3. As dissected by Veenhoven (2007), the HDI focuses on living conditions (in terms of material wealth), abilities (in terms of education level) and results or outcomes (in terms of life expectancy). Veenhoven is critical of it, though, as a measure of well-being. He says that it mixes apples and oranges – for example, chances of a good life are indiscriminately added to outcomes (ibid.: 227). There is also the point that as a benchmark it gives little indication of the degree of inequality (Phillips 2006: 7).

Overall, the breadth of the concept of well-being can be appreciated from a recent attempt to take an overview. Well-being is depicted as complex, determined not only by the resources that individuals have at their disposal but by the living conditions and societal processes they are exposed to and the decisions they take (Searle 2008: 30). One of the insights yielded by this broad approach is that quality of life

---

Box 2.3   UN's Human Development Index (HDI)

The HDI combines three dimensions:

Life expectancy at birth, as an index of population health and longevity
Knowledge and education, as measured by the adult literacy rate (with two-thirds weighting) and the combined primary, secondary and tertiary gross enrollment ratio (with one-third weighting)
Standard of living, as indicated by the natural logarithm of gross domestic product per capita at purchasing power parity

is a function not just of outcomes (which partly reflect the choices people make) and subjective assessments (which partly reflect people's adaptation to the circumstances in which they find themselves) but also resources (the factors that condition and facilitate such choices) and constraints in the various arenas in which people operate (Fahey et al. 2003: 16). In addition, a broad understanding of resources is offered. The opportunities open to people are brought into the picture, as well as the choices that they make.

There are three critical issues about well-being from the perspective of this book, however. First, as a general concept well-being is not underpinned by a firm conceptual base or an articulated theoretical framework – much of the push towards the concept is driven by an empirical set of interests (Allin 2007). Secondly, the scholarship does not generally identify the processes at work in well-being. The understanding offered of 'people in context' is quite rudimentary – even in its broadest meaning it proceeds with a rather general sense of the impact of surrounding conditions on a person or action (Megone 1990: 28–9). Thirdly, well-being is rooted in an individualist position. The causal arrow refers in the main to individual characteristics and experiences. Even when broader institutional areas and dynamics are included, the driving interest is in how these affect individuals. Hence, one can say that the well-being perspective lacks a sense of causal agency on the part of institutions or processes – it has little or no conception of the things that are 'done' to people. Where are social control, discrimination and stigma, for example? As Dean (2010: 88) says of Sen's capabilities concept, it is silent about the systemic impediments to human freedom that are associated especially with capitalism.

Care and Personal Relations

But we cannot and should not just park well-being and leave it. This is true for two reasons. First, we will continue to encounter some of the key ideas in well-being since they have penetrated quite widely and have close affinities with other areas of work. Well-being, it turns out, has been part of a paradigm shift which has involved much greater focus on the micro or individual level. As a consequence, it is now received wisdom that subjective aspects have to be set alongside objective situation for research on well-being to be credible. Moreover, the move to well-being represents a thrust towards multidimensional conceptualisations that is to be seen in the rise of other concepts also (e.g. social exclusion, which we shall consider below). A second reason not to jettison the well-being approach is that it has useful elements and tendencies. Jordan (2008a), for example, views it as the counterposing concept to economic welfare and utilises it to build an expansive critique of economic welfare. On the basis of well-being he draws up a reform programme based on quality of experience and what he calls 'social value', by which he means the cultural and institutional characteristics of human flourishing. He is interested in a different kind of order to that of the conventional economic model, founded as it is on materialism, contractualism and individual utility. For Jordan, a model based on a culture of respect and support is one in which emotions, personal relations and informal support are recognised as key elements of the social fabric.[5]

Here Jordan is picking up on a burgeoning literature. This is the scholarship on care and respect which speaks to both our intimate lives and our social relations. The 'ethic of care' scholarship maintains that an overlooked source of welfare and well-being lies in our personal moral identity as expressed in our orientations to others and especially our willingness to adopt a caring approach to those we love and those in need. The orientation and agency shown by people to providing and receiving care in the sphere of intimate relations has been depicted as inherently different to other forms of engagement (Tronto 1993; Feder Kittay 1999). Over time, this largely feminist literature has built up a body of work that emphasises the uniqueness and complexity of care, as a relationship, a set of activities, and a set of values and way of being (Daly and Lewis 2000). In the latter regard, care has been developed especially as a moral perspective in which people employ a moral reasoning about 'ought' and 'should' rather than an instrumental economic rationality of quid pro quo (Irwin and Williams 2002). It is also, though, very much a perspective about people's agency, and the activities and relations they engage in as part of their every-day lives.

The concept of care extends the meaning of welfare or well-being in a number of ways (box 2.4). In the first instance, our welfare hinges critically on the kinds of care we receive when we need it, both physical care and emotional sustenance and support. This is the customary meaning of care – servicing the needs not just of the young, those who are ill, and elderly people and others who cannot take care of themselves but also those who are able-bodied. Welfare in this view is the meeting of needs. Sociologically, one of the most interesting aspects of care is that it combines love, labour and ethics (Graham 1983). As labour, it invokes material circumstances, conditions of existence and an activity where women especially are involved (Finch and Groves 1983: 3). As love, caring draws upon emotional bonds, moral orientations and identity. As an ethical practice, care requires from the caregiver the characteristics of attentiveness, responsibility, competence and responsiveness (Tronto 1993; Held 2005). It may be liberating or constraining and is typically characterised by combinations of feelings of obligation, pressure, reward, commitment, trust and loyalty.

To recognise the second sense in which care extends our understanding of welfare requires that we move beyond a perspective that views care as confined to the settings and relationships connoting need, obligation and dependency. Seen in broader terms, a focus on care emphasises the relational foundations of all social life. There is no place here for solo individuals. Rather, key elements of people's welfare inhere in their relations with others and the reciprocity around responses to need and the receipt of recognition and value

---

Box 2.4 Two meanings of care

Care as providing emotional and other forms of support to loved ones and/or those in need
Care as social connectedness, as engagement with and commitment to general goals and principles around the quality of relationships

for who people are. No metric prevails. This extension of the meaning of welfare views care not in terms of meeting need but as an orientation towards both self and others. Among other things, care shifts the focus from general rules to actual relations of mutual responsibility and contributes to the development of a set of moral principles that focus on actual relationships rather than general or abstract relations (Gilligan 1982; Tronto 1987). The idea of caring about is important here also – caring about the environment, the welfare of animals or some political cause, for instance. It also involves taking responsibility (Tronto 1993; Sevenhuijsen 1998). The reference is not just to how we respond to the needs of intimates but how we view strangers and intimates alike. To be able to recognise this may require that we change our understanding of how we function and, instead of seeing ourselves as independent, view ourselves and those around us as interdependent and vulnerable (even when able-bodied).

Of course, the foregoing is in many respects an ideal and does not conform to the hard reality. Available evidence suggests that in practice care-giving and -receiving are often demanding, tedious, lonely and under-resourced (Lynch et al. 2009). Think of the pressure on the average parents of young children today, trying to fit in caring for their children around demanding employment schedules. Or equally, think of the work and stress involved in caring for someone with Alzheimer's disease or multiple sclerosis. Care relations are also a site of relations of power and they can be and often are part of a system of social control. There is a third caveat also which is that access to and involvement in care are also quite unequal. For example, care has been identified as a basis of gender inequality in that it is mainly seen as a female responsibility. Inequality in care arrangements is also to be found across socio-economic classes whereby those with most money have a choice of care options unlike the low income sectors (UNRISD 2010). There is also global inequality in that women migrate from the poorer countries to provide care in the richer countries (the 'care chains' of nurses and nannies and housekeepers) (Yeates 2004). Two underlying points about care remain, however. First, it is an inextricable and frequently overlooked domain of and approach to life that shapes and contributes to welfare and well-being. Secondly, not alone does it bring the so-called private sphere into focus but it leads to an analysis of everyday relations that views them in terms of negotiation, struggle and need fulfilment (Dean 2010: 96).

In the next and last section of the chapter, we range broader still and look to societal structures and processes and their implications for how we should conceive of welfare.

Welfare and Society: Sociological Theorisations

Welfare has not been central to the theoretical project of sociology and lacks a strong identity and 'home' in that discipline. Yet some of sociology's key concepts inhabit terrain that is constitutive of welfare and there is no doubt but that sociology overall has much to say about welfare. One of the most relevant contributions of sociological theorising is how it turns the attention to social and societal processes of integration and detachment. Concerns with material subsistence are framed in a larger context of social and economic processes, concentrations of power, and cultural processes.

To cut a swathe through a large volume of work here, I am going to focus on three concepts: poverty, social exclusion and social capital.[6] Table 2.1 sets out the main features of the three concepts in relation to each other.

Poverty is a concept that has undergone considerable change if not transformation since its early days (as sketched in the last chapter). One could capture much of this transformation by observing that poverty conceptualisation is becoming more and more 'socialised'. Of signal importance in this regard was the work of Peter Townsend in the 1970s and 1980s. Townsend's approach was heavily sociological – he was interested in the meaning of poverty and he believed that poverty could only be understood in terms of customary standards of living and the normal life of society. One of his seminal insights was that income as a measure of standard of living was flawed (Searle 2008: 16). Moving away from a purely economic conception of poverty as living below a minimal income threshold, Townsend (1979) argued that

Table 2.1   Key features of poverty, social exclusion and social capital

	Poverty	Social exclusion	Social capital
Focus	Access to material resources and standard of living	Normative and participative engagement	Connectedness in networks/ exchanges, trust
Dominant orientations	Distribution of income and resources	Cumulation of 'social problems' and disadvantages	Social progress
Purpose of concept for policy	To identify the distribution of people on minimum income/resources	To (re)frame social problems and promote welfare state reform	To instrumentalise social relations for economic growth and democratic functioning
Desired outcomes	Poverty reduction and alleviation	Included individuals, cohesive societies	Facilitated collective action, economic growth, democratic functioning
Empirical operationalisation	Income levels, access to a range of material resources and components of lifestyle	Persistent poverty, long-term unemployment, degree of involvement in social relations and political processes	Quantity of memberships, attitudinal measures of trust or corruption, involvement in networks

Source: Adapted from Daly and Silver (2008).

people's experiences of poverty differed according to how needs were conditioned by the society in which they lived. Poverty represented a 'lack of resources to participate in activities and obtain the living conditions and amenities which are customary or are at least widely encouraged or approved, in the societies to which they belong' (1979: 31). The idea of poverty as exclusion from the customary lifestyle of one's peers was born – and has stuck. This turns the attention to non-monetary indicators of living standards and to deprivation (or well-being) as defined by what is considered the norm in society. It counteracts the tendency in a poverty-line approach to cut the poor off from the rest of society. Subsequent work, especially in a broad European (including EU) context, has sought to develop poverty measurement along three lines. First, poverty is considered in subjective terms, conceived in terms of what people view as the necessary constituents of a reasonable standard of living (Mack and Lansley 1985; Van den Bosch 2001). This is a similar 'take it to the people' kind of approach as represented in the work on subjective well-being. Secondly, poverty is conceived on the basis of actual style of living, measured in terms of people's typical patterns of consumption and their household facilities (Gordon et al. 2004; Whelan and Maître 2009). This kind of thinking has opened the gates for the inclusion of many new factors in poverty measurement and for regular updating of the constituent measures.[7] Thirdly, poverty research has become temporalised, concerned with duration and especially the persistence of poverty over time. In sum, it has become the norm in Europe for poverty to be conceived and measured in three-dimensional terms – income plus measures of consumption and lifestyle (admittedly still quite rudimentary) plus duration.

However, poverty measurement is not socially contextualised everywhere. Conceptualisations of poverty in the US could not differ more from those in Europe. In the US an absolute income standard is used – a poverty threshold is set by the federal government which is calculated on the basis of the income needed to purchase a minimum dietary set of foodstuffs, goods and services.[8] The assumption is that families typically should spend about a third of their income on food and the calculations are made on that basis. Philosophically, it rests on the view that there is an absolute core to poverty which is linked to not being able to subsist or meet basic needs. An idea of intolerable hardship underpins it. Hunger is a benchmark here, as is being clothed, sheltered and free from disease. This narrow income standard approach does not include other aspects of economic status, such as material hardship (for example, living in substandard housing) or debt. Nor does it consider financial assets (including savings or property) or lifestyle or subjective factors. The contrast with Europe is stark – there poverty is almost never now measured by a sole measure of income and certainly not by an absolute income standard.

It is not such a long step from a relative view of poverty to seeing it as a form of exclusion. Social exclusion, a concept that has achieved some prominence in both sociological and social policy circles in Europe, stresses the processes engaged in (or not) by people rather than just the resources available to them. It is especially oriented to people's active participation in a range of spheres of life. As a condition or state experienced by people, social exclusion is characterised by a strong sense of dissociation, polarisation and isolation, the antithesis of membership and belonging (social inclusion). The concept's origins are diverse – for example, one can find traces of it in the ideas of the classical sociologist Emile Durkheim about different modes of social integration and 'anomie'. It also chimes with aspects of Amartya Sen's approach, especially in its interest in agency. The more proximate origins of the concept of social exclusion are in French social policy in the 1970s where it was used to describe people at the margins of society.[9] As it established itself especially in Europe over the course of the 1980s and 1990s, social exclusion came to have a diverse set of meanings. In policy circles it channelled the fear that people are becoming disconnected from both core networks, such as family, friends, social group, community, and core value systems (Silver 1994). A more critical interpretation roots it in social change and contemporary society – social and economic institutions are criticised for their failure to effect social integration, especially in a context of deindustrialisation and changing economies (Paugam 1991). It refers to society's broken promises in a way. The concept's implied need for institutional redesign and modernisation appeals to the European Commission, which has become one of the concept's strongest promoters and sponsors (Daly 2006). The underpinning vision of unity and oneness also speaks to the EU's project of political and economic integration of Europe. That said, social exclusion is lodged in quite different paradigms and discourses (Silver 1994; Levitas 1998). It is something of a chameleon concept in that it can play host to quite different analyses and competing social reform projects.[10]

While one can argue about the merits of the concept of social exclusion and whether it is new or not,[11] the concept offers some important insights about welfare. These become clear when one compares it to poverty (although it is important not to overdraw the comparison, not least because poverty research is taking a more dynamic turn and also because the concepts are not in competition). A defining element of the social exclusion approach is its sense of cumulation of different conditions of disadvantage – social, economic, political and even cultural factors are all involved. The concept seeks to pick up on the extent to which different types of deprivation interact and cumulate over time. It takes forward the idea of multiple layers or levels of disadvantage or 'diswelfares', although work has yet to render a satisfactory empirical account of just how different elements cumulate (although see Burchardt et al. 2002; Gordon et al. 2004; Levitas et al. 2007). Secondly, social exclusion brings a relational orientation (giving the concept some affinities with care). The social exclusion approach is underpinned by an ideal of each person being part of a diversified set of social networks in which they feel not just engaged but also obligated (Spicker 1997). 'Participation' is valued here, not for the capitals yielded but because it indicates agency and integration on the part of people. But there are weaknesses and uncertainties in the concept also. Of these I want to highlight three. First, it is not clear where the perspective locates causes and in particular whether it lays the emphasis on structural factors – such as inequality, for example, or people being denied the opportunities to become included – or individual behaviour. There is no doubt but that part of the concept's origins lie in a problematisation of the widespread experience of risk and marginalisation caused by increasing marketisation of society and a weakening of the earlier institutions and compromises of the post-war welfare state (Rustin and Chamberlayne 2002: 5). This predisposition towards structural factors can be and has been superseded by an individualist interpretation, however. In policy circles especially, social exclusion leads rather quickly to a project of labour market inclusion of the marginalised. Secondly, even though the concept has an all-society remit, it tends to be focused on the study of the poor and marginalised (as in EU usage, for example). Hence, while theoretically social exclusion refers to processes that are at the centre of society, in practice it is focused on the minority who are at the margins. This is probably related to the third weakness – it is not clear where the concept stands on social inequality, and in particular whether inequality is to be conceptualised in the traditional terms of class divisions or whether this has been replaced by new forms of inequality.

The scholarship on the third concept – social capital – speaks less directly than that on social exclusion to welfare but it is centrally interested in how people's social contacts and networks constitute a form of social capital and hence affect their own welfare and that of the community and society. At its simplest, social capital refers to the beneficial outcomes generated by people's propensity to associate together on a regular basis and to engage in civic and communal affairs.[12] Writ large, social capital picks up on the patterning of social relations, levels of trust and associational and other forms of participation and how they affect progress and functioning at a range of levels (from individuals to families to communities to social and political institutions). Social capital alerts us not so much to how people 'care' about or for others as to the benefits that accrue to them and others from certain cultural characteristics such as trusting attitudes, civic engagement and participation in social networks. The concept makes us take a fresh look at voluntary exchanges and informal social interactions in families, groups and associations. Whereas the care literature and even that on social exclusion would value these in their own right, social capital sees in them a type of resource with implications (see table 2.1). These are welfare-conferring not necessarily for themselves but because of the types of capital that they generate. Robert Putnam (1993, 2000) for example, one of the foremost promoters of the concept, is interested in assessing the relationship between the community stock of social capital (and especially the level of people's civic engagement) and progress (success) in democracy and/or the economy. Social capital in this view is either a kind of social glue holding groups, communities and eventually society together or a social lubricant making sure that people can interact with each other smoothly (Phillips 2006). Social capital is also, though, involved in 'diswelfare'. The French sociologist Pierre Bourdieu (1985) spotlighted the role of social capital in an unequal society, showing how it contributes to and reflects the prevailing power structures in society, especially in regard to how elites seek to maintain their privilege. For Bourdieu then, unlike Putnam, social capital is not a public good or a resource for integration at the societal level but a mechanism that serves to define and reinforce boundaries between groups and inequalities in society overall. The overwhelming resonance of social capital in public and academic discourse, though, is as an asset to be protected or harvested and a resource to be manipulated in the service of improving democratic and/or economic functioning. Communities that mix together accumulate together. If we were looking for an application of the approach, this kind of emphasis is to be seen in the work of the World Bank, especially in the 1990s. As a development tool, it used the concept to mobilise civil society and 'private' relations and resources for the purposes of improving the functioning of the market and good governance. Studies sponsored by the World Bank are especially interested in the positive effects of social capital, many being organised as case studies of grassroots institutions, such as rotating credit associations or micro-enterprises, self-help opportunities for the poor, and participation of the poor as part of 'good governance' (Narayan 2000).

Overview

By way of summarising, let us note some underlying tendencies, although we have only been able to skirt a very large literature. First, there is greater interest than heretofore in individual processes and in people's emotional life. The spotlight is trained on personal well-being in terms of desire fulfilment and emotional stability. Well-being as a concept is not focused solely on individuals' mental orientations, however. There is a strong interest also in individuals' capacities for action, the extent to which people have the resources and freedoms to make choices and realise outcomes which they consider valuable. Secondly, contemporary scholarship draws relational aspects of life to the fore and invites us to consider how features of interpersonal relations can be welfare-conferring. The field of care views this in terms of offering and receiving support whereas the concept of social capital takes a more instrumental approach and focuses on the benefits and advantages conferred by features of social organisation, networks and relations. Third, conceptualisations of social exclusion and a more complex view of poverty focus on the impact of the maldistribution of resources and the role of societal institutions and personal behaviour in generating inclusionary and exclusionary processes. Table 2.2 summarises the focus of each of the concepts. The complexity of human well-being is obvious.

Table 2.2 Emphases and interests of the concepts considered in this chapter

Concept	Main focus
Subjective well-being	Individual feelings, mental state
Well-being	Individuals' resources, capacities for action
Care	Personal relations, meeting of needs, orientation to others
Poverty	Financial and lifestyle inadequacy vis-à-vis others
Social exclusion	Exclusionary structural processes, individuals' level of engagement and participation
Social capital	Resources made available by social networks, cultural attributes and patterns of participation and engagement

In a more critical vein, certain things should be noted about the different concepts and developments in the field more broadly. For example, well-being (especially in its subjective meaning) has a strong individual connotation. While it prioritises the hitherto ignored subjective aspects of welfare, the turn to well-being tends to individualise conceptions of the human condition. The abiding interest is in the individual, and to the extent that social conditions are considered it is in the guise of factors affecting individuals' frame of mind or capacities for action. The concept also lacks critical intent. It seems to be driven by the search after positive experiences and ends and has less interest in how the wider environment generates negative experiences and outcomes. Social capital has similar kinds of strengths and weaknesses. Both concepts share an inherent idealisation of stability and harmony and convey an understanding of the well-being of individuals, groups or communities as embedded in some naturally occurring process of relatively benign evolution. Neither has direct terms to deal with divisive social phenomena and in this they represent a very different approach to, say, poverty or even social exclusion (in its more critical variants). The latter perspectives are grounded in a social problems orientation and they are in essence critical concepts. This means that like welfare they share a critical stance on the state and society.

One should not see the choice of concept or approach as random. At issue is a choice between positive and negative approaches which links into broader paradigm preferences. The popularity of well-being is part of a broader movement in scholarship towards the individual and towards an approach that emphasises agency as against structure. How concepts relate to broader paradigms and the values they carry exert, therefore, important underlying influences on whether the focus is on well-being and happiness on the one hand or poverty and welfare on the other.

What is notable about all of the scholarship considered in this chapter is that welfare as a concept is virtually absent. It seems old and jaded beside the fresh appeal of well-being. It is interesting to juxtapose the classic conceptions of welfare (as outlined in the last chapter) with the more social and individual-oriented concepts discussed just now. Although a good deal of the new scholarship is prosecuted in the interests of understanding individual (and sometimes internal aspects of) functioning, much of it also turns attention to relational and societal factors, showing how significant social relations and social resources are or can be for individual or societal welfare. This takes us some way beyond the conventional orientations to welfare. As Jordan (2008a) says, well-being requires a social explanation, lodged as it is in social relationships rather than in the classic economic model's understanding of welfare as lying in individuals and their material possessions. Taking on board the insights from the scholarship just reviewed, then, requires that we take forward an understanding of welfare that is focused on both: (a) material resources and related processes, activities and structures, and (b) the interpersonal and relational processes through which people give meaning and value to each other and to what they do. Hence, the meaning of welfare is to be broadened beyond the economic or objective to make it more relative and more social.

Intermezzo

As a concept or idea, welfare is framed and fashioned also in political discourse and contestation. It is an idea and a goal embedded in ethics and philosophy, in political organisation and in state practices. Not alone have philosophers and political theorists debated the meaning and constituents of welfare for centuries but countries across the developed world have organised and re-organised themselves for at least the last sixty years in the aim of achieving 'welfare' for their populations. The next two chapters turn to systems of political thought and practice around welfare. In the first welfare is examined by virtue of how it is framed in political philosophy; the second considers welfare as the object of state policy and societal organisation.

Chapters 1 and 2 have shown that the spectrum of ideas involved in or invoked by welfare is not only wide but also profound in terms of the depth of the issues involved. In chapters 3 and 4 we encounter further aspects of this depth when we turn to the politicisation of welfare. This takes us further into normative and prescriptive terrain, although the approaches to be discussed are also analytic in nature. The division of labour between the two chapters is as follows. Chapter 3 examines welfare as it is framed and contested by the dominant political philosophies and the next considers how it is organised under the auspices of the welfare state. Both chapters share an interest in identifying and analysing how long-standing positions are being rethought.

3

Classic Political Philosophies of Welfare

With a focus on 'ideologies and welfare', we engage here in a discussion of how the normative and political settlements around welfare are conceptualised by a range of political philosophies and political projects. The aim is to provide an account of the main theoretical frameworks within which political perspectives on welfare are formulated, and to get a sense of what is seen to constitute social progress and how these views are being rethought. There are three things the chapter seeks to accomplish. The first is to focus closely on the specificities of welfare as a contested philosophical ideal. How do differing philosophical positions frame welfare and how do views of welfare connect to core principles such as equality, liberty and justice? The place of welfare in liberalism, democratic socialism, Marxism and conservatism will be discussed in turn. Secondly, the chapter needs to clarify the main variants in perceptions of the relationship between welfare and forms of political organisation. The second part of the chapter, therefore, considers how these different views are rendered as perspectives on the organisation of welfare. It elaborates on the models of welfare that flow from the different theoretical positions especially with regard to the role of the state. The first two parts of the chapter show that welfare rests on a platform of associated ideas around which there is considerable disagreement. The third and final task is to outline how the different positions are being reframed in the light of changing economic and political circumstances. The logic of the chapter, then, has three layers: first the general philosophies, then the political versions of these philosophies as they view the appropriate organisation and form of welfare, and third change and reform.

Main Relevant Philosophical Traditions

There is a wealth of scholarship which has focused on the theoretical underpinnings and core ideologies of social policy (e.g. Drake 2001; Fitzpatrick 2001; Deacon 2002; Fitzpatrick 2005) and/or the links between different welfare policies and political ideologies and movements (e.g. Room 1979; Mishra 1990; Taylor 2007). As Jayasuriya (2006: 15) among others points out, ideas of welfare are not a free-floating set of traditions that can be cherry-picked. Rather, they are tied to large political projects of democratic evolution, market development, group well-being, political contestation, societal progress, citizenship and statecraft. Looking at welfare through the lens of liberalism, democratic socialism, Marxism and conservatism captures the breadth of thinking, positions and critiques involved.[1] Although popular debate tends to represent them in simplistic terms, the different approaches are not necessarily oppositional. They shade into each other in key respects, although each commands a distinct body of ideas. It must also be acknowledged at the outset that all of these are in themselves complex perspectives. The limited space available here allows us only to outline their general orientations and main tenets as they are relevant to a consideration of welfare. Table 3.1 presents an overview.

Liberalism

Many of the core ideas and concepts in liberalism are familiar from contemporary political culture and discourse. There is a lot of confusion about liberalism, though, not least because the adjective 'liberal' is used very generally. In a sense this

Table 3.1 Relevant emphases of different philosophical traditions

Perspective	Main focus
Liberalism	Individual autonomy and choice Market exchanges the best source of welfare Equality understood in formal terms as equality before the law Civil and political rights are the predominant forms of rights
Democratic socialism	Individuals and groups seen as political actors within the democratic state The state is the major provider of welfare, directly and indirectly Social as well as civil and political rights are essential Equality is understood as related to outcomes Social justice and social rights are emphasised
Marxism	Primary interest is the relationship between the state, the economic system and the system of ideas Critical of both market and state – seen as inextricably interconnected Welfare state serves functions for capitalism not least in contributing to the exploitation of the working classes Focuses on political mobilisation and ideological change
Conservatism	Focuses on individual and communal activities and forms of organisation Welfare resides in traditional forms of community and society The role and autonomy of family and informal institutions is vital Duties and obligations are emphasised Equality is conceived as equal access and fair procedures

wide usage reflects the fact that liberalism covers a broad spectrum of ideas. John Gray ([1989], cited in O'Brien and Penna 1998: 16) suggested that we should speak of liberalisms, the plural reflecting that it is a collection of related philosophies. These centre on the roles and functions of individuals, groups and institutions in managing, directing and controlling the character of human social life.

Individual freedom or liberty is a basic tenet of all strands of liberalism. People should have the maximum possible choice over their life and property. They should be free to pursue whatever it is they desire and use their resources as they wish. People's capacity to reason and to exercise choice in fulfilling their needs is also foundational to liberalism. If the moral sovereignty of the individual is the first principle of liberalism, the ideal of the self-regulating, market society closely follows. Beyond this, liberalism lacks a developed concept of society. Following Adam Smith, the 'invisible hand' of the market will deliver social well-being through countless, self-interested decisions which constitute the daily round of free market functioning (Turner 2008: 23). Society, then, is a by-product of individual activity. The role of the state is viewed through the prism of individual liberty and market functioning. Small government is preferred, especially by libertarians (radical individualists) who believe that the function of government (and citizenship) is to ensure basic civil protections and political rights – basically the conditions necessary for freedom of action. Welfare in liberal philosophy is not something that is provided but is achieved through the free and uncoerced actions of rational individuals (O'Brien and Penna 1998: 43–4). It is optimally located in a market context, for a number of reasons. People are the best arbiters of their own needs and so welfare organised by the state, especially in its universalistic variant, is inevitably paternalistic. In any case, there is no objective theory of need which could validate the collective supply of goods such as education or health (Barry 1999a: 59).

The variant of liberalism just described tends towards the libertarian side of the continuum. More social variants of liberalism also exist – these are more sympathetic to welfare as a matter of public concern. New liberalism, as represented for example in the work of T. H. Green (1906) and L. T. Hobhouse (1922), recognises the need to ameliorate the 'social problem' and promotes the idea of a common good as something more than aggregated individual satisfactions. For Hobhouse, progress is to be achieved through increased individual self-realisation, a process demonstrated by citizens' growing acceptance of the link between their own welfare and the welfare of others. The state has a vital role to play in the creation of such an altruistic society. The role of the state is especially developed by Rawls (1971), who in his liberal theorisation of social justice sets down the conditions for a social role for the state. This starts from a concern about the distribution of opportunities and how well society treats its worst off. A just society according to Rawls would involve the maximisation of equal basic liberties where the liberty of one person would not conflict with the liberty of others. Rawls's concern is with the distribution of what he calls 'social primary goods' – these are goods which every rational person can be assumed to want. They include basic liberties, freedom of movement and free choice of occupation, powers of offices and positions of responsibility, income and wealth and the social bases of self-respect. Such primary goods are for Rawls the basis for making comparative assessments of relative welfare – it is these which tell us how well people are doing (unlike Sen who as we saw in the last chapter sees capacities for action rather than goods as the measure of well-being). Rawls believes that these primary goods should be equally distributed, but he adds an important proviso: unless an unequal distribution of any or all of them would be to the advantage of the least favoured. Inequalities can continue to exist; they are acceptable as long as the institutions that produce them are open to all (equality of access or opportunity) and the inequalities also profit the disadvantaged.[2] A typical justification here is that inequality leads to economic growth which can benefit all. For Rawls a theory of justice has to be based on a view of society that everyone can share. This view, he thinks, is one of society as a fair system of co-operation between free and equal persons. Justice, then, is a system of fair rules within which individuals with different ends can co-operate to their mutual advantage (Sugden 1993: 1957). Justice is procedural rather than substantive, about processes rather than outcomes (Frankel 1966: 163). Equality too is viewed by Rawls in a relatively procedural manner – equality before the law, equal civil and political rights and in its more social variants equality of opportunity in the sense of removing barriers to personal advancement (Kearns 1997: 22). The state, especially in terms of law and the courts, has a key role here.

Democratic Socialism

Democratic socialism offers a political theory of welfare based around collective, democratic engagement. It is most commonly associated with the centre-left, social democratic political parties in Europe and as a model of welfare has been realised to the highest level in the Scandinavian welfare states (Lister 2010: 36–7). Both its democratic and social orientations distance it from liberalism. However, it shares common ground with liberalism in its commitment to individual liberty and rights and its capacity to live with the institutions of markets and private property.

A starting point is the state – democratic socialism views the state as a positive force in modern societies, one with a unique potential for benevolence (Kearns 1997: 12). The state is also seen as a site of power. The democratic state, as realised by parliamentary democracy, is the voice of the collectivity and is in many ways its guardian. First, the growth of state-organised systems of welfare is associated with the democratic process and especially the strength of working-class political mobilisation. Organised welfare systems owe their existence especially to the political agency of working-class actors, organised through political parties, trade unions and other political movements (Korpi 1983). On the face of it anyway, it is these sectors who have most to gain from the welfare state – although there is much research to suggest that actually the middle and upper classes gain hugely from the welfare state (Goodin et al. 1987). Secondly, for democratic socialists welfare – and state activity towards realising it for the greatest number possible – has meaning mainly in terms of fellowship with and solidarity among the working class. The state has another meaning also in democratic socialism – the nation state. Welfare provisions organised by the state serve a nation-building function, leading not just to a sense of common purpose among the people but to an improvement in the national stock of human capital and a means of differentiating those who belong to the nation and those who do not (Williams 1989).

The state's role in conferring welfare by meeting need is more or less undisputed in this perspective – this is a minimal state function. Democratic socialism makes the case for a much more extensive welfare conferring role for the state – it should be an instrument or agent of progressive social change. A redistributive role for the state – especially in regard to material resources – is essential if it is to correct for the inequalities generated by the market. The required forms of intervention extend across economic and social policies and beyond liberalism's narrowly conceived welfare policies (Deakin 1994: 10). Different justifications have been offered for why equality should be a goal of social policy. Following Fitzpatrick (2001: 23–4), these rest on two basic types of argument. One is the acceptance that as humans we all share basic needs, indicating the presence of some common basic nature – as we saw in chapter 1 Doyal and Gough (1991) suggest health and autonomy as two basic needs that people have in common. A second justification is more explicitly normative: that fairness and social justice require equality and a commitment to a fair distribution of social resources. Thus, in the long view, the state should act to equalise life courses, not alone giving security when the market is unable to provide it but also undermining the inequalities that stem from birth, inherited wealth or economic power. In addition, the institutions and processes associated with the welfare state serve a socially integrative function – they are both constitutive and expressive of community. The ideals of community penetrate quite widely in social democracy. It emphasises especially fellowship and solidarity – in the sense of common cause with others (even at the expense of one's own interests) and the good of the community as a whole (Spicker 1991). Welfare is not monopolised by the state therefore – social democracy also recognises the role of voluntary provision and 'self-help', although the state's is the dominant role.

Marxism

Marxism is rooted in an analysis of the organisation of production, the systems of economic, social and political relations to which it gives rise and the mechanisms that perpetuate them. For Marxism economic relations of production are interwoven with a set of political, ideological, social and cultural practices. This forms the integrated 'whole of society' (Lavalette 1997: 53). In Marxist terms, capitalist societies are class societies which are conflictual in nature given the exploitative relations that exist between classes. Marxism devotes considerable attention to state-organised welfare. While there is no single Marxist theory of the state, it is as a perspective highly critical of social policies and rejects the benign implications of the term 'welfare state'. Social policies are a response to the problems created by the structure and operation of capitalism in the area of labour reproduction especially (ibid.: 63). They are therefore instrumental. Given this, the state is neither neutral as in the liberal view nor benevolent as in the democratic socialist perspective. States cannot be separated from societies nor from the economic and political relations associated with the economic system. The state in Marxist analyses is wide-ranging and ubiquitous: it includes the legislature, the civil service, the judiciary, the army, the police, various local and regional organs of government and a range of other quasi-autonomous, semi-public bodies (ibid.: 63). According to Offe (1984), social policy provides for the transformation of work into wage labour in three main ways:

- Institutions and processes of socialisation (e.g. schools, training and so forth) provide the motivation for workers to choose wage labour over alternative means of subsistence.
- The range of health and social services and also income supports provided when people cannot work or are preparing themselves for work enable people to reproduce themselves as fit and able workers.
- Through its various regulatory mechanisms the welfare state intervenes in the labour market to balance the demand for workers with the supply of labour.

Looked at from this perspective, then, social policies are a means of maintaining the status quo of unequal and exploitative relations and structures characteristic of capitalism. Social policies also serve to discipline and control particular groups within society, especially the poor (Piven and Cloward

1971). Not only does the welfare state shore up capitalism but it legitimates it as well. The existence of the welfare state even when it is a response to the demands of the working class is essentially a form of perpetuation and legitimation of ruling class domination (Gough 1979). But having to accommodate these divergent requirements also renders the welfare state contradictory (Offe 1984) – a precarious balancing act of conflicting interests the welfare state is quite unstable. A Marxist social policy is premised on the abolition of private property and exploitation of labour and the self-fulfilment of each individual and the entire society through creative and free labour (O'Brien and Penna 1998).

Conservatism

Conservative understanding of welfare focuses closely on society. In this it differs from the individualist focus of liberalism and the political/economic focus of both democratic socialism and Marxism. Where liberalism emphasises the rights of individuals, conservatism sees the world in terms of the obligations and duties of community membership. For many conservative thinkers – especially those who are communitarian in orientation – liberalism is too atomistic (Taylor [1995], cited in Dwyer 2000: 30). Society needs rules to function and the ways that have evolved over time have a kind of natural logic to them. As outlined by Pinker (1998: 65), conservatism has two outstanding characteristics. First, in starting not from the formulation of abstract principles but from the reality of established institutions such as family, community, religion, private property and government, it privileges order and continuity and sees these as resident in existing institutions, practices and beliefs. Secondly, conservatism views society as organic, formed by the gradual evolution of accepted institutions which exist in a complementary relationship. Traditional values and practices represent accumulated knowledge and adaptations to best practice – they have already proved themselves. One has to add a third characteristic to conservatism also – its underlying belief in the priority of morality and morals (Nisbet 1986). Conservatism sees society as having a natural moral order, unlike individuals. The perspective is, according to Lister (2010: 30), premised on a pessimistic view of human nature as inherently imperfect. Conservatism certainly is heavily invested in behavioural assumptions – something it shares with liberalism. Unlike liberalism, though, conservatism believes in strong authoritative government. It is less sure that welfare should be one of the state's primary functions, though. Welfare is seen especially in terms of the, typically organic, solidarities and practices generated by tradition, family, neighbourhood, status and nation. Conservatives are not opposed to state-organised welfare in principle but they are conscious of the need to protect social life from political 'interference'. The natural harmony of stable hierarchical community must not be disrupted by the welfare state or other forms of the political state. The duty of the state in regard to welfare is to protect and buttress these solidarities and generate a moral commitment to them.

Models of Organised Welfare

The political philosophies just outlined represent to varying extent 'pure' positions. When philosophy meets politics, the philosophies are honed by political processes and the harsh reality of political projects and contestation. The four political philosophies feed into and come together in specific visions or configurations of organised political and social life. With this we are getting closer to the institutional arrangements for welfare that exist in countries (the subject of the next chapter).

Following Dean (2006: 21–4), two axes usefully capture the main variations involved when it comes to how these political philosophies are translated into a set of principles and arrangements. The first is a liberal–republican axis which involves distinctions between positions on individual liberty on the one hand and those on social solidarity and community membership on the other. The second axis spans conservative and egalitarian ideologies, distinguishing between approaches that seek to preserve the existing social order and those that are in favour of addressing inequalities. The four quadrants are displayed in diagrammatic form in figure 3.1. Each suggests a different model or version of welfare as a set of organised principles.

In the first quadrant there is the social liberal approach which more than any other was the signal influence on the post-Second World War welfare state according to Dean (2006: 22). William Beveridge, the architect of the post-war welfare state in the UK, for example, is a major figure in the social liberal perspective, as is Franklin D. Roosevelt. Social liberals have faith in individual autonomy and regard the free market system as the best way of organising an economy but they believe that both individuals and the economy need managing and that government has a role to play in such management. For social liberals, it is both necessary and possible to graft measures of state welfare onto capitalism, to soften its 'rough edges' (George and Wilding 1993: 46). Gradually increasing welfare for all fits in with their conception of society as dynamic progress towards an overall human destiny. Procedural equality of citizens should not be compromised (Dean 2006: 22). The law (and the state form based on it) must, therefore, provide due process in the sense of

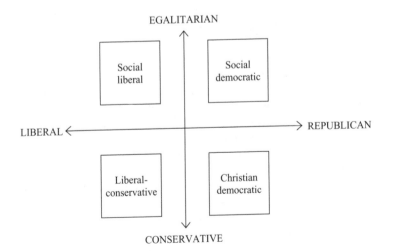

Figure 3.1   Main perspectives on organised welfare

both protecting people from injury and giving them a procedure for redress should their rights be infringed. Procedural equality is close to the idea of equality of opportunity. Viewing equality in individualistic terms, the aim is to furnish a fair basis for managing inequalities, by strengthening the minimum to which everyone is entitled and by using equality of opportunity to regulate the competition in the search after scarce resources (Baker et al. 2004: 25). The conception of equality as opportunity is mainly concerned with the progressive removal of legal impediments to participation (such as in work or education). Non-discrimination is one of the classic remedies to inequality of opportunity in the social liberal view. Individual and group differences are not a problem in this view as long as basic rights and equal status of citizens are respected. Equality of welfare, then, means that we as individuals (are enabled to) attain our preferences and the things that matter to us to fulfil our needs. The goal is not equality of outcome but a social minimum for every citizen. Not so much social justice as fairness should prevail (George and Wilding 1993: 67) and any social rights granted must be congruent with market functioning rather than working against it (Fitzpatrick 2001: 129). While there is a notion of social progress through social intervention, individual liberty is an ongoing concern, as is maintaining the divide between public and private and ensuring that the latter thrives.

A second approach is egalitarian/republican in nature. It is a close rendering of key elements of the democratic socialist philosophy outlined earlier. It is really only from this perspective that we can speak of the welfare state which is seen as a 'significant post in the transition from *laissez faire* capitalism to socialism' (George and Wilding 1993: 74). Social justice is a guiding moral principle and so measures are justified on that ground rather than in terms of liberty or fairness as in the liberal conceptions. The welfare state is socially just in that it is: (a) concerned with outcomes (as against the process or procedure of much of the liberal theorising) and (b) specifically redistributive: 'it defines fairness not in terms of an allocation of economic resources tied to individual entitlements under the procedural rules of legitimate ownership but as a complex set of institutions designed to take account of "needs" and "deserts" that transcend claims based on private

property' (Barry 1999b: 2). This state is interventionist and
seeks to effect social justice by addressing and redressing
social class disadvantages and inequalities through the granting of social rights. Social citizenship – in the Marshallian
sense of strong social entitlements – is well established, and
by granting people rights to income and services when they
need them the welfare state sets itself between the individual
and the market. This kind of welfare state model is a guarantor and even purveyor of welfare in terms of a more equal
distribution of economic resources. Welfare here is an ideal
of compensation and redistribution in accordance with a
perspective on equality as equality of outcome. The manifold
benefits perceived to be associated with the welfare state
include the abolition of poverty, the promotion of economic
growth, fulfilment of individual abilities, promotion of social
integration, encouragement of altruism in society, and reduction of inequalities (George and Wilding 1993: 82–3).

Thirdly, there is the conservative/republican approach
which is socially conservative but committed to some collectivism. This has strong Christian democratic resonances
and religious roots and is quite familiar in Europe although
not in the UK or the US. The German welfare state is the
exemplar here as are other states such as Austria in what
Esping-Andersen (1990) has denoted as the 'continental conservative world' (which will be outlined in the next chapter).
The corporate nature of society and organic interdependence
of different sectors is emphasised (Van Kersbergen 1995). All
the major power holders – government, employers and
workers – are given a say in decision-making and there is a
strong emphasis on negotiation and consensus among the
conventional power holders. The 'disadvantaged' are to be
treated with compassion but the objective of organised
welfare is to preserve the status quo rather than to change
society. Hence, traditional values, systems of authority and
long-standing institutions, such as the family, civil society, the
professions and religion, should not be undermined by state-
promoted welfare provision. Indeed, they should be allowed
to develop organically and so the welfare state should support
them. 'Family values' and 'back to basics' are familiar terms
in the mouths of proponents. It is not just a question of
values, though. These other institutions apart from the state

are seen as the best providers of welfare – they should have the first crack at it – and they are especially preferred over the state (via the principle of subsidiarity which gives precedence to the lower-order institutions or spheres) (Spicker 1991).

The final variant – in the conservative/liberal quadrant – is most familiar as the liberal-conservative approach associated with Margaret Thatcher in the UK and Ronald Reagan in the US in the 1980s and much earlier in the Poor Law in England. It is an ideologically-driven position, associated especially with the growth of the New Right,[3] which achieved prominence as an intellectual and political force in the 1970s and 1980s and has since held the spotlight very effectively. This approach combines strong support for the market and a view of social order that is seen to be best served by the preservation of tradition and the status quo. State power should be harnessed to instil moral values and shape individual behaviour. A clear public/private divide is favoured – it does not totally reject a role for the state in welfare but the general attitude to the idea of state-organised welfare is one of suspicion and anxiety (George and Wilding 1993: 20). The goal of welfare policy should be growth and wealth creation rather than equality. A kind of a trickle-down position is taken which views economic growth as benefiting all. In this view growth is more likely to enhance national welfare and to make society more equal than any egalitarian policies (ibid.: 24). The relief of poverty is the most legitimate function of the welfare state. The perspective eschews any real concept of inequality as social and is not led by a strong conception of social justice.

Changing Perspectives and Priorities

These perspectives have been subjected to varying interpretations and they have been challenged, not least by perspectives and/or political movements that point out key weaknesses and negative outcomes for particular groups. For one, social divisions other than those based on social class or economic position (which is the primary division dealt with by the classic perspectives) have been highlighted. The classic perspectives have been accused of being gender and race blind, of ignoring divisions based on gender or those arising from racial faultlines (Wilson 1977; Williams 1989; Skocpol 1995). Feminist work especially critiqued the failure to take into account the fact that the classic models all rested on a sexual division of labour that was unjust to women (Pateman 1988). There is also the matter of race and ethnicity – the classic perspectives show little understanding that their models are built on homogenous conceptualisations of the population and that terms like 'the state' and 'welfare' are far from neutral from a race and ethnicity perspective (Williams 1989). A related critique is that forms of identity other than those within the dominant cultural perspective are not actively considered by any of the classic welfare models. The perspectives remain quite impervious to these and other developments, although in aspects of their organisation welfare states have responded to these critiques, to some extent anyway (as we shall see in the next chapter).

So how are the perspectives changing? The two axes used to frame positions on welfare (figure 3.1) can also be used to illustrate how the classic perspectives are being revised. It should be noted that the revisions, too, shade into each other in key respects and that each of the perspectives has a number of sub-strands which we only touch on here. Figure 3.2 therefore is meant to indicate broad tendencies and should be treated with care.

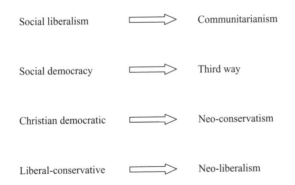

Social liberalism ⟹ Communitarianism

Social democracy ⟹ Third way

Christian democratic ⟹ Neo-conservatism

Liberal-conservative ⟹ Neo-liberalism

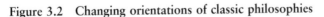

Figure 3.2   Changing orientations of classic philosophies

The social liberals have turned to community. Modern communitarianism emerged in the 1980s as a response to what its advocates saw as the excessive individualism bequeathed by a resurgent liberalism (and the work of John Rawls (1971) in particular) in the US, the UK and elsewhere. Communitarians tend to look backwards and, when they do, today's society is seen to compare unfavourably with that of yesteryear. Things have become unbalanced and in particular society's intermediary structures – family, religion, civic associations – have been undermined. Etzioni's (1995) metaphor of the three-legged stool gives a good sense of communitarianism's critique of society. The two legs constituted by the market and government, he says, are longer than the third leg of community and civil society. Communitarians worry especially about the moral basis of organised state welfare (Taylor 1989; Walzer 1990). At the core of communitarianism are three beliefs (Deacon 2002: 65–6). The first is a conviction that freedom should never be confused with self-indulgence. This means that individuals need to practise self-restraint and that societal agencies need to provide governance in that regard. Individualism and self-interest must be curbed. The second is the belief in the existence of a common good or public interest over and above the private interests and personal goals of individuals. It is the common good that makes freedom possible, and actions are virtuous or otherwise depending on their contribution to the common good rather than how they benefit individuals (Fitzpatrick 2001: 64). Thirdly, communitarianism holds that individuals possess a moral sense which disposes them to make moral judgements and to heed the judgements of others. However, they need to be helped with the acquisition of appropriate moral habits. The welfare state, therefore, needs to be re-envisioned and reworked so that its central objective is to enforce social norms and expectations and to give effect to moral actions on behalf of the community. Communitarian welfare would not take people as it finds them but would try and change them, emphasising especially the obligations of individuals, the importance of social order and the worth of traditional values and ways of life (Deacon 2002: 76). The virtues and values of civil society and the 'informal web of social bonds and moral voices of the community' – which are essential to a communitarian understanding of welfare – are not promoted sufficiently by state-organised welfare (Etzioni 1998). These traditional values and institutions are where an ethical basis for politics and individual behaviour is to be found (Prideaux 2005: 98). It will be seen that communitarianism has some common ground with the concept of social capital considered in chapter 2 in that both emphasise the virtues and benefits that flow from informal social activity.

Social democracy, too, has shaken itself down and begun to re-envisage the relationship between welfare and capitalism. The old democratic socialist approach is considered no longer feasible, mainly because the economic and political conditions that underpinned it no longer prevail. Hence, in a climate of globalisation left of centre governments feel that they have less leverage than heretofore; in the realm of democratic politics people seem less likely to vote along class lines than they did in the past. But it is not just a question of scarce resources or changes in politics: ideologically contemporary social democratic theorising has turned critical of the welfare state itself. This critique is captured well by perspectives that fall under the rubric of the 'third way'.[4] This kind of approach to policy and politics is probably best exemplified by the policies of the New Labour government under Tony Blair in the UK between 1997 and 2007. Lister (2010: 48) sums up the position by saying that it is pro-market and ambivalent about the state. It has certainly made a virtue out of the necessity to accommodate to global market conditions and to adjust the social democratic welfare state and its regulated labour markets accordingly (Ryner 2010).

It is, therefore, less critical of capitalism than the classic democratic socialism and less interested in effecting major corrections to the market. Instead, it turns the spotlight on individual and collective responsibilities and duties (e.g. Commission on Social Justice 1994). Sociologists have made a signature contribution – especially Anthony Giddens (1998), who has utilised an analysis of risk in the context of postmodern societies to retheorise social democracy and redesign the welfare state. He develops the idea of positive welfare which has meaning only in contradistinction to negative welfare – the classic welfare state that aimed to provide security to people over the life course may have overprovided in that it has made people passive and dependent. Giddens considers that in these high-risk, very changeable times people need to possess a capacity for risk taking so that all can participate in the wider economic system. Decommodified welfare – the system of granting people generous benefits with few if no conditions around employment attached – increases moral hazard,[5] in the sense of people reneging on their responsibilities (Ryner 2010). The nature of government must, therefore, change. There are different labels for the new welfare state model – some people call it an enabling state while for others it is a social investment state.[6] Regardless of how one names it, in the new social democracy the state is a facilitator of economic participation rather than a social protector. Supply-side policies offer labour-market training and tax breaks for childcare and pension savings as a quid pro quo of people assuming more responsibilities (ibid.). The contrast to the classical social democratic philosophy is striking: it saw compensation, redistribution and demand management as the primary purposes of the welfare state (Jayasuriya 2006). New social democracy, says Fitzpatrick (2001: 19), is not concerned with inequalities *per se* but with unjust inequalities – those that fly in the face of effort and desert. Equality is defined not in terms of the possession of an average complement of resources but as a matter of enabling and supporting individual capacities and fighting the most blatant 'exclusions' (ibid.: 41). Redistribution, formerly an end in itself, becomes a means to an end of enhancing capabilities as welfare is more and more framed within the market. We can even see concepts from sociology deployed in this new ideology. Social inclusion and social capital become goals of social policy, and in this and other ways welfare state programmes are more closely linked with wider economic ends.

Neo-conservatism has an even stronger critique of state welfare, much of it morality- and culture-based and some of it shared with communitarianism. From the 1970s on, it took command of the conservative discourse on welfare by pursuing a mainly moral critique. This rests on the belief that a stable society, and an efficient market system, depend on the 'internalisation' of appropriate norms of behaviour by all citizens (Barry 1999a: 78). Conservatives take aim at the welfare state especially because of its social and cultural consequences – the changes in 'character', the 'dependency', and the corrosion of both moral standards and a naturalistic self-reliance that a too-generous welfare state might induce (ibid.: 55). The institutionalised welfare state leads to bad habits ('dependence' especially), displaces authority, undermines the family as a collective unit, and creates 'disorder' in society (Murray 1984; Mead 1986). Neo-conservatives have been labelled 'anti-modernists' in that they regard social progress, and in particular the destruction of tradition by modernisation, as a major social and political problem (Rodger 2000: 21). Foreboding is in charge here and the old certainties of traditional life are preferred. While the welfare state is dismissed as too paternalist, governance is an underlying interest of neo-conservatism. Reminiscent of Michel Foucault's (1991) concept of 'governmentality', neo-conservatism endorses behavioural regulation through directive social programmes and strengthened supervision and surveillance so that people – and especially the poor – can be shown how to take personal responsibility. In the US, neo-conservatism goes so far as to favour the removal of disruptive individuals through incarceration (Western 2006; Fording et al. 2009; Wacquant 2009). Between 1970 and 2003, state and federal prison populations grew sevenfold, with most of the growth occurring among poor, uneducated minority groups – people who are otherwise likely to be claiming 'welfare' (Western 2006). Work enforcement, though, is the preferred activity over incarceration since work is the most fundamental social obligation of citizenship and an indispensible starting point for a well-ordered life (Fording et al. 2009: 7). One can see some of these concerns already in the fledgling Conservative–Liberal Democratic government in the UK. David Cameron's 'Big Society' programme, in particular, pits the state and a very simplified notion of society in competition. The problem is that the state has too much authority, reaches too widely and is morally corrosive, so it needs to be countered by 'people power'. It is planned to turn the state into a zone of quasi-private activity. 'Society', in the guise of individual volunteers, is to be given the power (and some resources through funds from dormant bank accounts) to take over the running of public services. This is a version of the ownership society – but rather than along the lines of the US model where people insure as private individuals in the market, citizens enact ownership of the local services and public resources.[7] This 'takeover' is also envisaged for public-sector employees who are to be encouraged to form workers' co-operatives. Before they are sanctioned (by the state presumably), all of the initiatives must be economically sound and may even function on a 'payment by results' basis. As Wiggan (2010) says, the move to empower staff and citizens would widen the reach of market rationality and contractualism and shift the state further towards the role of purchaser and away from that of provider.

And finally there is neo-liberalism. Emerging from the liberal traditions of the past, neo-liberalism became increasingly popular during the second half of the twentieth century. In fact, the influence of neo-liberal and neo-conservative thought and policy throughout the 1980s, 1990s and 2000s in the UK and the US was so strong that it shifted the political centre of gravity around the welfare state and related issues to the centre right (Rodger 2000: 97). The connection between classic liberalism and neo-liberalism rests in large part on the moral critique of the state and a reiteration by the latter of possessive individualism and the freedoms associated with private property, market relations and trade across nations (Fording et al. 2009: 2). Neo-liberals such as Hayek (1960, 1976) and Friedman (1962) were dismissive of the managed economy advocated by Keynesianism. They saw it as part of a larger collectivist impulse that was threatening to devour the philosophy of individual freedom (Turner 2008: 63). Neo-liberalism's origins are rooted here: it developed as a defence of capitalism and free-market economics in fierce opposition to socialism and collectivism (Braedley and Luxton 2010:7). Neo-liberalism reserves particular fire for the crises seen to be generated by the social democratic welfare state. Such crises are defined to include rising unemployment, balance of payments deficits and an increasingly costly public sector. In its suggested solution to these crises, the logic and practices of the market are to be extended as widely as possible – it is these that guarantee the freedom of individual agency that is so prized by liberalism just as the state damages it. Market rationality is the normative ideal to be achieved through public authority and the state is a site for the application of market principles.

Contrary to popular opinion, then, while neo-liberalism's critical focus is the state, it aims not so much at weakening the state as changing it. 'Welfare' in the neo-liberal view requires a revitalisation of market relations, a subordination of everyday life to transactions in a regulated economy (O'Brien and Penna 1998: 103). From a welfare perspective, neo-liberal reform puts its faith in the effects of incentives and disincentives, especially as they are expressed by the system of benefits and taxation, in changing individual and collective behaviour. In neo-liberalism, social justice lacks specificity and legitimacy as a concept and goal. There are many possible criteria of social justice (need, merit, desert and so forth) but in a free society there can be no general agreement about which of these should be used for resource allocation (Pratt 1997: 42). As we shall see in the next chapter, there have been three key neo-liberal principles as they have been incorporated into welfare: the idea of inclusion within the economic mainstream of all citizens; the growth of privatisation and market-based forms of provision; altering the operation of the welfare state so that it enhances people's human capital resources so that they can compete more effectively in the market economy (Jayasuriya 2006: 20).

Overview

This chapter has shown welfare to be loaded with political meaning. It rests on a platform of philosophies and discourses which propound different visions of what is 'good' and 'right'. Welfare, therefore, picks up on and serves to define fundamental aspects of these philosophies. As a political ideal, welfare is, at one and the same time, an expression of moral responsibility and a component of systems of political beliefs about such matters as the relative primacy of individual freedom over collective goals, the nature and role of the state, the extent to which the operation of the market and the economy needs direction and governance, and the role and place of intermediary institutions like family and civic associations. The range of positions on these matters taken by the classic philosophies is striking.

However, when one lays out the dominant discourses of reform side by side it is remarkable how much common ground they share and how narrow is the field of debate nowadays. For one thing they all subscribe to the idea of the market as a disciplinarian and provider. Moreover, they favour increasingly exposing people to the market as a source of welfare while gradually pulling away or thinning to a thread the safety net which people assumed would be there for them if they needed it. Secondly, they are all committed to accommodating the changing nature of market conditions – only social democracy has a critique of global capitalism and financial markets but it, too, ultimately favours accommodation and only weak regulation (as has been laid bare in the response to the latest recession). Thirdly, all the perspectives put great faith in intermediary institutions. For neo-conservatism the family looms large among these but it shares with reformist social liberalism a strong commitment to community. Even social democracy now is an advocate of community and it, too, subscribes to the belief that a too generous welfare state is corrosive of human motivation and responsibility. Fourthly, there is a wide consensus on the failings of the welfare state. In some quarters, the critique is hostile. Over time, then, revisions in the classic perspectives, which in the past had a stronger independent identity, have brought them closer together – so much so that they agree on much of the canvas of reform. Even such a crisis as the latest recession has not engendered much in the way of new debate or change of positions. The huge investment in fiscal stimulus in 2009 seemed to presage a Keynesian response but as time has gone on it has been revealed that the 'adjustment' is at heart neo-liberal and neo-conservative.

The next chapter considers actual welfare state arrangements within and across countries. We shall see that what have been presented in this chapter as relatively coherent sets of ideas have not anywhere seen the light of the day in their pure form. Implementation is messy and political ideology and expediency tend to select out the particular ideas or programmes that suit the moment, regardless of whether these are philosophically coherent or not. Neither are decision makers averse to combining together emphasises from perspectives that rest on or draw from different philosophical foundations. All of this makes really existing welfare states quite different to ideal models.

4
The State and Public Welfare

This chapter focuses on organised systems of welfare as they have evolved in Europe and the US. Here we get into the detail of welfare systems that were sketched as philosophical models and political orientations in the last chapter. The welfare state is the lead concept. The chapter addresses three sets of questions. First, how is the welfare state defined and structured and how has it evolved? The relevant discussion gives an overview of how welfare states conceive of and seek to effect welfare and the significance of the accommodations involved with the market, the family and personal life and society more broadly. Second, how do welfare states differ from each other and how are such variations to be explained? Using a comparative approach, the discussion here draws a series of broad profiles of how 'welfare' is interpreted as a public responsibility and operationalised in a range of countries. This treats of the classic differentiations between welfare states (namely, liberal, social democratic, conservative). Thirdly, how are welfare states being reformed? Change and possible transformation are the focus here, especially in light of the many factors pushing for reform.

Defining the Welfare State

The welfare state is a particular form of the state. Titmuss (2001) traced the earliest usage of the term in Britain to

William Temple, then Archbishop of Canterbury, in *Citizen and Churchman* (1941). Temple used the idea of the welfare state normatively – for him it was an alternative to the conception of the power state of the dictator. In Temple's view, the term 'welfare state' held only if the state fulfilled its moral and spiritual functions in promoting human welfare. The concept also informed wartime debate in Europe and to a lesser extent the US. In Germany, the concept connoted a sense of disparagement – the Weimar Republic was retrospectively attacked in the 1930s for being a *Wohlfahrtsstaat* because the excessive social 'rights' and expenditure it had endorsed ultimately destroyed its legitimacy (Lowe 1999: 3). The preferred German term was and still is *Sozialstaat*. The latter was perceived in a more positive light as conveying a sense of entitlement to public benefits but also a set of social concerns. But from the middle of the twentieth century on, the term 'welfare state' has become part of the mindset and everyday lexicon in Europe and elsewhere. It is associated with notions of concerted state action and a social compact which involve entitlement in case of need or desert, social betterment, especially of the working classes, and a range of institutions and services oriented to meeting need.

A number of terms take us into the territory of the welfare state: social security, social policy, social welfare. We could use any one of these but the welfare state is a superior concept in a number of respects. In the first instance, it is a theoretical term, invoking theories of power and how authority and control are vested in the state and utilised by it in a diversity of ways.[1] The welfare state concept also possesses the idea of a comprehensive system or model of provision oriented to social planning. Rationality is a strong underlying belief. The welfare state, therefore, picks up on a formative idea in Western Europe especially, whereby the nation state embodies a form of administrative rationality and individuals overcome their alienation through projects of collective actors aspiring to change the social system (Albrow 1993). While there was certainly an evolutionary aspect to it, in many countries the welfare state was introduced, in the Second World War period, as a decisive intervention to combat existing ills. In the UK, for example, William Beveridge (1942) conceived of it as addressing five giant problems in the context of the society of the time: want, idleness, ignorance, squalor, disease. Inherent in the welfare state concept, then, is an idea that is rationalist in nature: it is a set of programmes and provisions with a job to do. The notion of regime, which has become a popular way of thinking comparatively about welfare states especially since Gøsta Esping-Andersen used it in his very popular book *Three Worlds of Welfare Capitalism* (1990), conveys a strong sense of system.

One can define the welfare state narrowly or broadly. If used narrowly, the term refers to the aims and objectives of publicly funded actions concerning social needs and the provisions through which such needs are met (along the lines of the social liberal or liberal conservative models outlined in chapter 3). Conceived more broadly, the definition offered by Asa Briggs (2000: 18) is evocative of the social democratic model sketched in the last chapter:

> A welfare state is a state in which organised power is deliberately used (through politics and administration) in an effort to modify the play of market forces in at least three directions – first, by guaranteeing individuals and families a minimum income irrespective of the market value of their work or their property; second, by narrowing the extent of insecurity by enabling individuals and families to meet certain kinds of 'social contingencies' (for example, sickness, old age and unemployment) which lead otherwise to individual and family crises; and third, by ensuring that all citizens without distinction of status or class are offered the best standards available in relation to a certain agreed range of social services.

There are a number of genuine insights here. The first is the idea of an intervention into and beyond the market – the existence of the welfare state is testimony to the limits of market outcomes even if at the same time it represents an accommodation with the market which seeks to alleviate its less defensible consequences. A second reference in Briggs is the idea of rights to income replacement in the event of being visited by certain contingencies, security if you like. Thirdly, social class inequalities are seen to yield to attempts to mitigate their worst effects. This was especially one of the hopes for the social democratic welfare state – the idea that the welfare state would build a common set of life chances above sectional interests and groups separated by inequalities but favouring those with fewer resources. Redistribution of income, access to services like education, housing and health, the creation of opportunities for advancement and the amelioration of inequalities were formative objectives in this regard. The welfare state, therefore, thematises some of the core structural themes of European sociology: class, the state and the individual (Albrow 1993).

Briggs's definition also indicates the normative foundations of the welfare state. Lodged in it is the conviction that societies can consciously put in place policies designed to eliminate 'abuses' if not 'wrongs' which in earlier generations had been accepted as inevitable (Briggs 2000: 19). In every country, the development of the welfare state was accompanied by strong moral argumentation, a flavour of which has been given in the last chapter.

Theoretically, it is helpful to treat the welfare state as a component of statecraft – the initiation and implementation of policies by political agents that elaborate and regularise fundamental relationships between the state and political groups (Malloy [1991], cited in Jayasuriya 2006: 148). It is helpful also, and one of the insights of this book, to regard the welfare state as embedded in society whereby it is itself both the product of social forces and a component of social relations, norms and social organisation. In practice, it rests on and comprises a broader set of relations than discussed in the last chapter – between state and economy certainly but also drawing in culture, community, family and society (O'Brien and Penna 1998: 1). This societal perspective allows us to appreciate how the welfare state (in all its forms) engages with social and personal relations and how it embodies economic, social and political ends which take effect in people's real lives (to be considered in chapters 5 and 6). It is a social as well as an economic and political institution.

The Evolution of Welfare and the State

In the course of the modern era, just as the vocabulary for discussing the issues of ignorance, poverty and disease gradually shifted from a religious to a political and social idiom, so too did organised provision become less local, less focused on need, less private and voluntary, and more national, universal, public and social.

In Europe and those other countries where it has been tried as a form of organisation, the welfare state has become a vast conglomerate of nationwide, compulsory and collective arrangements to remedy and control the effects of adversity and inequality (De Swaan 1988: 218). To merit the name 'welfare state', provision needs to be of a certain scale. This takes time to evolve. European and American welfare programmes were, in fact, a relatively long time in the making and so the term 'evolution' better captures their emergence than does 'revolution'. As a rule, the 'take-off' period for state-organised social policy in Europe tended to predate the full post-Second World War flowering of the welfare state by close to half a century. Prior to this, welfare in the sense of 'external' help was largely purveyed through face to face, highly localised relationships within the medium of what we now call 'civil society' (Ritter 1986; De Swaan 1988; Harris 1992; O'Connor 2001; Fraser 2009). Welfare-related activities historically were motivated in the main by either charity, religious duty, a tradition of self-help or some kind of collectivist orientation (as in trade union benefit funds, for example). Activities oriented towards welfare, especially in the early days, were centred on a process of creating and revising the moral and other classifications of the poor (Handler and Hasenfeld 1991). The stigma on the pauper class was important in view of the ever-present danger that this class would expand at the expense of those considered 'deserving poor' (widows and children, for example) (Teles 1996: 2–3). Hence, a major change in social ideas and their political application was a necessary condition for the welfare state to emerge. Ritter (1986) shows that in Britain from the end of the nineteenth century *laissez-faire* ideals and the belief in the individual's ability to improve his or her situation through own effort increasingly gave way to more socialist and collective attitudes (described in the last chapter). This paved the way for the new social order – which stretched temporally from the New Deal or post-war period to the 1970s and 1980s. Social democratic in orientation, its main social feature was a class compromise, between managerial and working classes, which involved the containment of capitalist interests (Duménil and Lévy 2009).

The welfare state, then, embodies a commitment to transfer some responsibility for welfare from individuals, families, communities and localities to the state and the public authorities. This has been nowhere a total transfer but to merit the title 'welfare state' the state must assume a major responsibility for the welfare of the population.

Germany led the European way by instituting in the 1880s social insurance as a means of dealing with the costs and consequences of industrialisation and of giving effect to Chancellor Bismarck's authoritarian desire to integrate the workers into the newly created federation of states (Ritter 1986). The German approach was for national, wage-related, compulsory, occupation-based social insurance (Jones-Finer 2004). By the turn of the twentieth century, Germany's model had caught the attention of other countries. Although not always in exactly the same form as in Germany, by the outbreak of the First World War in 1914 no fewer than fourteen European countries sported some form of statutory social insurance programme (ibid.: 12). The 1920s saw growth of provision for widows and families, reflecting the devastating effects of war, and during this and the following decade the experience of mass unemployment spurred most European countries and the US to add unemployment to the list of risks covered by social insurance. Typically, the early forms of social insurance were organised either directly by the state or indirectly under public auspices, delivered through employers or workers' organisations. Social insurance is notable for many reasons, not least that it collectivises risk. So, for example, if you become unemployed and you are insured, the benefits to which you are entitled will be paid out of the contributions of those who are working. Collectivist in orientation although governed by market principles, it could not be more different to the systems of poor relief that it replaced. In effect, certain risks of income loss are rendered social risks – attributed not to personal shortcoming or 'natural causes' but to social factors. Moreover, they are seen to happen to 'us' rather than to 'them'. Before we get too warm and fuzzy about the bonding implied by social insurance, however, we should remember that social insurance is underpinned by the cold rationality of contract. It represents a bargain struck between groups with often opposing political interests and enforces obligations around working and claiming entitlement for example (Jordan 2008b).

In the immediate post-war period, European states concentrated upon extending social insurance, centralising the administration of services and benefits (from the voluntary and occupational sectors), introducing cash benefits to support families with children and instituting a network of social services to raise standards of health, education, housing and general welfare. Once the economic hardships of the post-war period had receded and economic growth and stability provided both the resources and the political demand, energies were focused on making social insurance benefits more generous, widening their coverage, universalising access to a minimum income safety net, and putting in place a set of social services and family supports. These post-war reforms were significant for many reasons but especially because they represented the first systematic attempt to apply the insights of social democratic theorists to the solution of social problems (Kearns 1997: 19). John Maynard Keynes had argued that managing the level of demand in the economy by controlling the money supply would enable governments to pursue full employment as a policy objective. William Beveridge similarly argued that with social planning poverty could be eliminated and that it was not an inevitable consequence of the economic cycles associated with capitalism. Full employment and social insurance would guarantee protection for virtually all citizens.

The Structure of the Welfare State

There are different ways in which to conceive of the welfare state. One of the most widespread is to take the broad parameters and constituent elements of provision – this is an especially popular way of organising comparative analyses (e.g. Esping-Andersen 1990; Sainsbury 1996). This kind of exercise usually focuses on the risks and contingencies that call forth financial or other forms of state support, the institutions put in place to deliver on the promises of collective welfare, and the kinds of political settlement implied by the arrangements that are in place. Some of the classic analyses here differentiate income/taxation from social services and within these broad categories the orientation of particular measures and services (e.g. old age support, family-oriented measures, unemployment, illness or disability, education and so forth). A useful way of analysing the constituent elements of income compensation is to differentiate between universalistic benefits (which are organised on the basis of social citizenship and are therefore available to all citizens), social insurance (which links benefits to contributions made through employment) and social assistance (which utilises a series of tests and thresholds to distribute benefits and services on the basis of need or perceived 'deservingness'). The relative prominence of each of these mechanisms goes a long way in indicating where the type of model fits in the quadrants of figure 3.1.

The welfare state must also be seen in terms of aims and functions, however. The most minimal undertaking of welfare states is the avoidance of poverty. To achieve this, safety-net programmes have long been a feature of the European model of society, and also that of the US. Such programmes usually provide an income floor below which no one is expected to fall and they are usually organised on a social assistance basis (which as mentioned above implies that tests or thresholds are applied to assess eligibility). But the citizen's guarantee from the welfare state (in Europe anyway) extends considerably beyond the avoidance of poverty, relating to unemployment, illness, accidents at work, pregnancy, widowhood or old age and increasingly the need to give or receive care (for children and the elderly). The list of contingencies covered by social insurance in the US is much smaller – in fact one could count them on one hand. Retirement, unemployment, disability or illness and in some cases medical treatment are the main risks covered there. The European model is more expansive in other ways as well. European welfare states also aim to support families with the costs of having and caring for children and they usually offer support to those who provide care for ill or elderly adults as well. One could say that they 'socialise' care to some extent. The interface between the employment system and the family is thus an important consideration for policy in many countries, with the EU and the OECD encouraging countries to offer leave from employment for family purposes and also more flexible working conditions (Lewis 2006; Mahon 2006). Apart from guarantees of financial support, nation states in Western Europe also assume responsibility for citizens' access to certain educational, housing, social and health services. While they may not always be the direct provider of these services, most states undertake to ensure that: (a) access is widely available; and (b) a satisfactory level of services exists.

To appreciate the full import of the welfare state it is helpful to put it in a broader context still. Robert Walker's work (2005: 43) is useful in illustrating some of the ways that welfare systems function at a micro as well as at a more macro level (see table 4.1). The scope and reach of the welfare state is quite remarkable. As Walker (2005: 31) describes it, welfare states bind diverse groups together in a web of mutual support and obligations that help to define the nature of citizenship, nationhood and national culture. While it is always something of an open question whether they achieve this, the welfare state is a major part of the status quo, and as such underpins and reproduces economic development and key aspects of the character of economic and social life. The package of provisions in place affects the whole life course, from cradle to grave. Social control emerges as a strong theme from table 4.1. In addressing 'social problems', social provisions frequently target the behaviour of individuals and particular sectors of the population for change. This, of course, means that welfare states promote certain values and in this and other ways act as agents of social control. Foucault's work (1985), which admittedly ranged broader than the welfare state, underlined how discourses based on dividing practices, often incorporating binary divisions among people or groups, are reproduced in state practices. Some of the key divisions with which welfare states work are: worker/pauper, healthy/unhealthy, deserving/undeserving, worker/non-worker, good mother/bad mother, law-abiding/delinquent (Leonard 1997: 50). Dean (2002), too, emphasises how the welfare state controls and contains. This control is often

Table 4.1   Functions of state-organised welfare systems for individuals and society

Actions	Aim/rationale	
	Individual level	Collective level
Provision for needs	Humanitarian	Social welfare
		Economic development
Maintenance of circumstances	Protection	Reproduction of status quo
Organisation of family life	Shape how people act as family members, and their propensity to engage with family	Social stability, organisation of gender and generational relations
		Management of care demand and supply
Development of potential	Affect individual capacity	Effect integration and equality
Changing behaviour	Reward Deterrent	Social control
Remedying disadvantage	Cure Compensation	Equality Social justice
Production of disadvantage	Control	Reproduction of social divisions (e.g. gender, ethnic/racial divisions, division among social classes)
Reproduction of values, culture	Perpetuation of norms and values	Reproduction, social control

Source: Adapted from Walker (2005: 43).

subtle in form (e.g. procedural rules, tests and penalties). Rather than viewing the welfare state universally in terms of control, though, it might be more helpful to see it in terms of a continuum. 'The typical form of intervention by the social welfare institutions of society moves from repression of negatively regarded "social problem" behaviour, through attempts at regulation, outright assistance in different forms, efforts towards individual rehabilitation and restoration to "normalcy", towards systems of preventive measures' (Pusić 1966: 84). In this and other ways, welfare provisions also serve to reproduce harm and disadvantage.

Welfare states, too, perpetuate tradition. This can be seen clearly in how social policies approach families and private life. For long, European welfare states supported a male breadwinner model of family life (Lewis 1992). This made a differentiation between women and men whereby he was responsible for earning and she for caring for home and family. There is a large literature to show that welfare state provisions, at least until the 1980s, acted to cement women's dependence on men rather than to undo or seriously challenge it (Lewis 1992; O'Connor et al. 1999; Daly and Rake 2003). In the last ten to twenty years, this has been eroded by an agenda around the organisation of work and family life which is much more favourable towards female employment (but is not necessarily supportive of equalising unpaid work between women and men). This has overseen the expansion of childcare and leave from employment for parenting purposes (e.g. maternity, paternity and parental leaves). Underpinning these and other reforms is a perceived need to manage the provision of care, especially in a context of demographic imbalances that are increasingly seen as hazardous for the sustainability of welfare systems (too few people earning and contributing for the numbers of elderly and others who are claiming benefits). Other faultlines of division, especially those of race and ethnicity, also underpin welfare states' design and operation (Williams 1989). As well as being overtly discriminatory in some contexts, welfare states carry forward assumptions about race (Lewis 2000). And it is a common pattern for people from particular racial or ethnic backgrounds to predominate in particular social programmes. The so-called welfare in the US, discussed in chapter 1, is a case in point, dominated as it is by people from minority groups.

Even though it is noticeably absent from Walker's political economy-oriented approach, it is incomplete to conceive of the welfare state without making explicit reference to it as a cultural entity (last row table 4.1). As a cultural form, the welfare state encodes social and cultural meanings through social policies in relation to roles, identities and relations as well as the conceptions of people as subjects (Clarke 2004; Van Oorschot 2006). Thinking of welfare in this way directs attention to how social policies seek to affect people's subjective and social identities and the linkages that they construct between people's sense of themselves and their social positioning. Among key dimensions here are the degree to which policy encourages or enforces norms and obligations around responsibilities with regard to employment and self-sufficiency, for example, and the legitimacy they give to particular roles, forms of living and lifestyles. In essence, there are symbolic codes embedded in social policy and in this and other ways social policies (seek to) engage in a cultural politics of representations and demarcations that rewards some forms of identity (e.g. worker) and marginalises others (e.g. full-time parent) (O'Brien and Penna 1998: 124). The welfare state is, therefore, a form of cultural intervention, and as we shall see later in this chapter welfare states are increasingly engaged in trying to shape people's identities.

Welfare State Variation

Following the discussion in the last chapter, it will come as little surprise that welfare states today and historically vary considerably from one another. Indeed, variation is so widespread that it renders discussion of *the* welfare state in generic terms somewhat imprecise. Nowadays it is very common to speak of welfare state types or regimes. The academic work of recent years makes a strong claim that European welfare states can be grouped into a number of base types or models (Esping-Andersen 1990; Lewis 1992; Daly and Rake 2003). While the designation of both nation and type tends to be controversial, most analysts would agree that the differences and similarities among welfare states in Europe are such that one can speak of a liberal model, a Nordic social democratic model, and a continental European conservative model. The models are differentiated from each other in key respects. Such differences reside not just in practical arrangements for organising and managing social security or philosophical orientation but in the nature of the role of the state and other institutions that are at some fundamental level concerned with welfare (like the family, civil society, the market).

Drawing upon the work of Esping-Andersen (1990) and Walker (2005: 14), table 4.2 sets out the characteristics of the different models schematically. These are broad models, ideal types really. Thinking in this way helps to organise the variation systematically, although it must be pointed out that these are to a large extent ideal types and so are only approximations of the arrangements that actually exist in particular countries.

One welfare state model is liberal in orientation. This will be familiar from the discussion in the last chapter and also from what happens in the UK and to a lesser extent Ireland. Further afield, 'liberal' is an appropriate descriptor of how welfare is organised and governed in Australia, Canada and the US (although there are very significant cross-national variations especially in terms of where the line is drawn between public provision under the auspices of the state and private provision).[2] This kind of welfare state is more indi-

Table 4.2   Characterising the main welfare state regimes

	Liberal	Social democratic	Conservative
Role of:			
Family	Marginal	Marginal	Central
Market	Central	Marginal	Marginal
State	Marginal	Central	Subsidiary
Civil society	Of some importance	Marginal	Central
Dominant model of solidarity/ citizenship	Individual-based	Universal	Kinship Corporatism Etatism
Dominant locus of solidarity	Market	State	Family
Degree of decom-modification	Minimal	Maximal	High (for breadwinners)
Characterisation	Residual	Universalist	Social insurance

Source: Walker (2005: 14).

vidualistic than collective in orientation and tends to support the market as the main means of resource allocation. Hence liberal welfare states are characterised by a low degree of 'decommodification' in the sense of welfare benefits which give people an income when they are not participating in employment. To the contrary, social policies strongly encourage participation in paid employment for all by offering mainly low-level welfare payments and attaching strong conditions to their receipt. The major goal of social policy in this type of welfare state is to combat poverty and meet basic need. The liberal welfare state model is generally less interventionist as regards improving the conditions of work (e.g. through minimum wages) and less overtly supportive of family life, as compared with other models. Among other things, this means that the state does not use its taxation and benefit systems to bring about wider goals such as gender and racial equality. The furthest this type of welfare state goes is to put in place anti-discrimination measures. This type of welfare state is, therefore, sometimes characterised as 'residual'.

By comparison, in the Nordic countries where social democracy is an enduring political ideology, the welfare state tends to reach very wide, intervening not just in the labour market but also in the family. The model will be familiar from the discussion in the last chapter. Universalism is a strong principle here – with social insurance extended to the whole population rather than just for wage earners and a wide network of social services in place. Provision in social democratic countries was born out of a mix of universalist and liberal principles which means that it prioritises paid employment for all but does so in a manner that values equality. This welfare model does not exclude those who are not earning, although it includes them on somewhat different and less generous terms than workers (which means that it has its own forms of gender and racial inequality) (Anttonen 2002). The social elements of citizenship are well developed here, including its strong sense of a national community (which makes provisions somewhat inhospitable to 'outsiders'). A commitment to equality, including gender equality, is deeply embedded in these countries and the prevailing model of citizenship aims not just for equality for women as workers and carers but also as citizens in the public sphere. In these mostly tax-financed welfare systems, the idea of a citizen's benefit is well established. As a consequence, these countries resist the idea of tailoring services to particular groups – the services and benefits have a strong sense of uniformity and are designed for all citizens (Sainsbury 1996). The degree of 'decommodification' is quite high, although most benefits take account of and require some period of labour market participation and are linked to wage levels. In addition, full employment was, up to recently anyway, a goal of government policy so that women were almost as likely to be employed as men and the state regulated for a wide range of childcare and other services and employment-related leaves to support this type of gender arrangement (Leira 1992). This makes for a smaller role than elsewhere for the family, kinship, community and the private sector in the provision of care and a larger role for the public authorities.

The continental European model, which draws Austria, Germany, Belgium, Luxembourg and partly France and the Netherlands together, offers a stark contrast to both characteristic liberal and social democratic welfare arrangements. This has origins in etatism (and in particular the attempt to use social benefits to foster allegiance to the state) and in religious (especially Catholic) and civic republican traditions. The model resembles the conservative model described in chapter 3. Rather than the universalism of the Nordic model, it is oriented to particular population sectors and the preservation of the status and other differences between different occupational groups. The classic social insurance model of risk pooling is widely accepted and is the basis of the model. This means not only that benefits have to be earned through employment – and that most people basically pay for their own benefits (or in the case of pensions for the benefits of the current generation of pensioners) – but that the level of income replacement depends on the height of the relevant wage or salary (which means the best paid get the highest benefits). Corporatism is the decision-making mechanism whereby representatives of the state, employers and workers decide on a 'social compact' (which encapsulates the main decisions around wage rates, employment regulation and changes to benefit levels). This too acts to reproduce the rewards that groups achieve in the marketplace and keep the system stable. The model does secure those at the bottom, though, through strong safety-net provision. This type of welfare state intervenes in the family only reluctantly. A key aspect of its conservatism is that it relies on a traditional model of family relations, encouraging married women and mothers to be carers (on a part-time if not a full-time basis) and husbands and fathers to be the main financial providers (Daly 2000a). However, there are variations in the family- and gender-related components of these welfare states, with France especially encouraging employment on the part of mothers, so one must be careful about generalising. Civil society organisations (e.g. NGOs) are valued as service pro- viders, although this too varies by country.

These three models do not exhaust the 'organised welfare universe' in Europe, however. Although it is in some ways a mix of other models (in particular the conservative and the liberal), there has been said to be a characteristic Mediter- ranean welfare state model as well (Saraceno and Negri 1994; Ferrera 1996). In Italy, for example, social insurance has a long history although it was mainly limited to public-sector workers. This, together with the fact that social service provi- sion is patchy, has led to a characterisation of the Mediter- ranean welfare state as 'dualistic' and 'under-developed'. The family plays a major role in welfare provision. The prevailing family model is traditional (especially in a gender sense) and also multi-generational.

There is also the, now defunct, communist model. This was a system where the state defined welfare needs and pro- vided for them, often through the medium of the enterprise or place of employment. In the former communist bloc coun- tries today, social policy is being refashioned, generally along the lines of a social insurance model. However, there are strong elements of residualism also. Poverty and basic needs tend to dominate and social insurance tends to be limited, both in extent and generosity (Castles and Obinger 2008). Because coverage is far from universal and has many gaps, private systems of support (especially the nuclear and extended family) are of high importance.

How did different countries come to have the welfare models they did?

Explanations for Different Models

It might appear from the last chapter that philosophical and political orientation is the main factor determining the welfare state. In fact, it is only one set of factors. Ian Gough (2008; see also Gough and Therborn 2010) speaks of five causal factors. His 'five I's' as drivers of welfare state development are: industrialisation, interests, institutions, ideas/ideologies, and international influences:

1. Industrialisation – changing economic, demographic and social structures
2. Interests – collective actors, power resources, class movements, political parties
3. Institutions – nation-building, citizenship, states, constitutions and political systems
4. Ideas – culture, ideologies, epistemic communities, policy learning
5. International, supra-state influences – war, globalisation, global civil society policy transfer, global governance.

Under the broad impact of industrialisation are such factors as changing economic, demographic and social structures. The growth of industrial capitalism tore apart old structures of support and generated the economic and other resources to provide new ways of dealing with welfare needs. By 'interests', Gough is referring mainly to the impact of democracy and party political and other forms of political action, especially on the part of different socio-economic classes. The underlying point here is of the welfare state as a class compromise – a set of arrangements that benefit the working class especially but are also to the benefit of middle and upper classes. Gough, thirdly, attributes importance to the development and then continued existence of institutions which especially strengthened the capacity of the state and the resources available to it (through raising taxes, for example). Nation-building was an important reason for welfare state development and it is notable that many welfare states in Europe were developed, initially anyway, in the context of colonialism. Creating a sense of belonging among 'insiders' (and equally excluding 'outsiders') lent many welfare states racial undertones (or even overtones in some cases). Fourthly, Gough views ideas and belief systems as foundational influences on the development of welfare states. Here he is referring to the part played by cultural systems, ideas and dominant ideologies (along the lines outlined in the last chapter) and policy transfer or policy learning. Gough's final 'I' is the international environment. Relevant factors here include the impact of war, globalisation and global governance and of policy transfer. These factors all interact.

When comparing the European experience to that of the rest of the world, Gough and Therborn (2010) point to three unique factors in Europe and the western developed world generally that aided the development of the welfare state. First, outside of the Mediterranean region, the western societies had the nuclear family system which meant weaker kinship ties and responsibilities and greater importance for occupational associations and territorial organisations, villages, cities and states (ibid.: 763). People could not rely on a wide kin network and so they had to create new structures of support. Secondly, the prevailing conception of rights, emanating from Roman law and reinforced by the canonical law of the Catholic church, located concerns about the well-being of the population and the administration of justice in popular claims and new institutions rather than lordly benevolence or charity. There is, thirdly, the fact of the post-Second World War boom which, lasting for at least twenty years, led to economic and employment growth and relative stability, hence giving a chance for the arrangements to establish themselves. Most of the non-western world has never experienced this kind of long boom period.

If the discussion in the chapter thus far portrays the welfare state as fixed or static, we must qualify the interpretation. Barry (1990: 43) suggests that the idea of the welfare state is a misnomer, that it is in reality a complex set of shifting, and often conflicting, normative viewpoints. This is an important insight, alerting us not just to the varied nature of state provision and organisation of welfare but also to the fact that it is subject to contestation and change.

Change and Reform

It is now widely agreed that welfare states are in transition
and that the characterisation given thus far in this chapter
may actually be historical in that it pertains to the golden age
of expansion of welfare states in the three to four decades
after the Second World War. Since the late 1970s, the dynamics of globalised capitalism and the spread of neo-liberalism
as the dominant ideology have been undoing elements of the
post-war welfare state models (Clayton and Pontusson 2000).
This has built up a momentum over time so that today a sense
of epochal change regarding the role and functions of the
welfare state prevails (Rodger 2000: 14). We are either at a
crossroads or have already taken a new route. At the minimum
the current times (which I define to include the last fifteen to
twenty years) are a period of transition.

The changes made to the British welfare state are instructive, not least because they reveal how some fundamental
issues about the role and scope of the welfare state arouse
controversy and even backlash. Its liberal model also carries
a lot of influence internationally (especially in the current
climate). Under the successive Conservative governments of
the 1980s and early 1990s, relations between individuals, the
state and the market were at the centre of reform. While the
changes are complex, one could say that the understanding
of the state's welfare-related role was moved closer to market
needs, market functioning and market norms in a number of
respects. A productivist ideology has been put in place in
which the role of the welfare state is increasingly to facilitate
employment and self-sufficiency on the part of individuals.
New Labour when it came to power in 1997 adopted many
elements of this philosophy while overseeing the expansion
of the welfare state, especially into services and economic
support for families with children and better provision in and
regulation of areas experiencing deprivation. According to
some, the unique contribution of the successive Blair governments was to present the objectives of welfare policy in positive, integrative terms rather than in negative polarising terms
(Brewer and Gregg 2003). For others, though, this smacked
of functionalism – seeing the entire social system, including

capitalism, as intrinsically harmonious (Levitas 1998; Prideaux 2005). The main problem for public policy in this view is of maintaining order and enabling the harmonious development of key institutions like family, school, community, and so forth rather than ridding the system of inequalities and other consequences generated by hierarchical power structures. At the risk of oversimplifying a very active social policy programme that spanned thirteen years, there were three overriding emphases in New Labour's social policy: a welfare to work programme, a child and family support programme, and a programme to tackle social exclusion especially at local neighbourhood level. All three were closely related, especially the latter two since for New Labour poverty in childhood is a key transmission mechanism of social exclusion and deprivation across generations (Deacon 2003: 66). Key elements of the policy package were closely influenced by the Clinton administration's approach to welfare put in place in the US in the 1990s – according to Gough and Therborn (2010: 765), this was the first real influence effected by the US on European welfare states.

What of the US then? Jacob Hacker (2008) frames the radical changes there in terms of a 'great risk shift', charting the erosion of social rights and collective assumption of responsibility for risks. Beginning from the 1970s, coverage of risks – which was never as extensive as in Europe – has been shifted away from insurance provided by government and employers and towards individuals and families who are increasingly required to self-insure through the market. In the US today, only around half of workers employed for more than twenty hours a week receive health coverage through their jobs. They must therefore buy health coverage if they can afford to. But the market is also dictating the type of coverage available. Hacker says that 'old-style' health coverage with no-money-down care and choice of physician is now virtually non-existent (2008: 36–7). Pensions, too, are also provided commercially and have been transformed from defined benefit to defined contribution. Today, less than a third of large- and medium-sized firms in the US offer a defined benefit retirement plan. Instead, there is the ubiquitous 401(k), which is akin to a private savings account. People are given tax incentives to save for their own pensions by investing in these special accounts, the yields from which depend largely on the performance of the stock market. The scale of investment in 401(k) accounts is equivalent to a fifth of the national economy (ibid.: 112). In this and other ways, the market controls more and more of the average American's current and future 'welfare'. Instead of being protected from the market – one of the key functions of social security – people are expected to seek protection in the market. The change has both economic and ideological roots. Economically, it is associated with the changing nature of employment and the growth in the private insurance industry and federal government support of the latter. Ideologically, neo-conservative discourses of 'personal responsibility' have played a central role in undermining public provision by virtue of its supposed moral hazards. The 'freedoms' supposedly conveyed to people when they are in charge of their own insurance in the private market are heralded. George W. Bush called it the 'ownership society', promulgating the notion that personal ownership is the only genuine source of social security and economic prosperity (Béland and Waddan 2007). Social insurance was cast as a failure, criticised for coddling the irresponsible and worsening the very problems it was meant to solve (Hacker 2008: 53). The consequence, as we shall see in chapter 5, is that short- and long-term insecurity as well as volatility in income is a common experience for the average American. At the same time there have been profound changes in the already residual 'welfare' or means-tested programmes. The 1996 United States Welfare Reform Act, a Clinton reform measure, shrank the number of recipients of the Aid to Families with Dependent Children/Temporary Assistance for Needy Families from over 5 million cases and 11 million persons in 1994 to under 1.8 million cases and 4.5 million persons by June 2006 (Munzi and Smeeding 2008: 33). It also shifted the nature of expenditure from cash aid to services (such as training) and made employers into major beneficiaries through tax credits. Fording et al. (2009: 15) make the important point that the extent of state intervention did not change in the US but what did was how the state was intervening, for what purpose and to whose benefit.

It is important not to be too focused on changes in the liberal welfare states, however. If we take as our vantage point welfare state provisions in mainland western Europe, it does not look like a moment of welfare state retreat, but rather of reorganisation. The state, as a 'guarantor' of rights and a funder although not always direct provider of certain services, is still a strong referent point in the lives of citizens and even in the discourse of centre-right governments. The evidence on how much change has actually been implemented in European countries is mixed. The general European pattern, to the extent that one can speak of such, is more one of gradual reform with old principles holding, although starting to give way, as changes in the global economy and political philosophies erode old settlements (Bleses and Seeleib-Kaiser 2004; Clasen 2005; Starke et al. 2008). Countries have been strongly encouraged towards reform by the OECD and the EU (Jayasuriya 2006). There is evidence of some shifting in the legitimacy of claims of particular sectors of the population. The needs of children and families have become more prominent, for example, and there is less sympathy for the unemployed and those who cannot be employed because of an illness or disability. Starke et al. (2008) conclude that there is no race to the bottom or indeed neo-liberal 'Americanisation' of the welfare state in Europe and that to the extent that countries with different models are converging it is a modest convergence towards the centre.

Examining programmes and expenditures only may be to look in the wrong place, however. It is instructive also to consider how the welfare subject or benefit recipient is being re-envisaged. Some of the changing philosophical ideas outlined in the last chapter are being implemented. The idea is widespread now that people have to take greater self-responsibility and that the state should not 'spoonfeed' people or enable them to pursue 'irresponsible' behaviours. Dependency is the mortal sin in this perspective. The new active welfare subject is a citizen, a consumer, a voter, a stakeholder, a worker (Williams 1999: 671; Jayasuriya 2006). She is also a partner in a contract that sets out her responsibilities and the conditions under which she may avail herself of public resources. There is greater concern about the behavioural implications of social provision and the assault against the underlying conditions that cause vulnerability is considerably weakened. It is the person and his or her choices rather than the risk that is being managed (Chamberlayne 1997). One way of framing all these changes is to say that citizenship is being flattened into an economic register (Fording et al. 2009). At the core of the new market citizenship and welfare governance are two neo-liberal concepts of welfare: the idea of 'inclusion' within the economic mainstream for all citizens, and economic independence and competition in a globalised market economy (Jayasuriya 2006: 20).

Overview

This chapter has considered the collective organisation of welfare. In Europe especially, the story is of the growth of the welfare state. All evidence points to the scale of welfare as an object of public policy – a huge edifice has been constructed to generalise welfare as a condition of individual and collective life. This has overseen the expansion of social insurance, taxation and a range of public services. It is also to varying degrees seen in interventions to 'humanise' employment and to curb the excesses of the market. However, it is also clear that countries have varying interpretations of what 'welfare' means, the priority that is given to collective welfare, and the kind of infrastructure and measures put in place to realise it. There are many perspectives, hopes and projects lodged in the developed welfare states.

It is also clear that we are in a transition and that the original 'golden age' of the expansionary and socially ambitious European welfare state is now behind us. Benefits are being cut back, there is a turning away from the level of taxation that is needed to fund the welfare state, and the virtues of market-provided services are extolled over public provision. In short, the acceptance of a social welfare role for the state is more and more queried. Yet, the welfare state has not been undone. To understand why and have a sense of what might happen in the future, it helps to regard welfare states as complex in origin and in operation. Gough's 'five I's' above (2008), suggest that the factors that fuelled the development of welfare states included changes in the economic and social situation, political engagement and mobilisation, institutional

development and expansion, ideas and international developments. The fact that we have moved away from some of the
underpinning conditions (like unequivocal political support)
should be kept in mind when considering the likely future of
the welfare state. So too should we be mindful that welfare
states are balancing acts. As mentioned, they developed out
of a class compromise and in their operation they balance
opposing ideas and interests. Jordan (2008a: 58), for instance,
attributes the longevity of welfare states to the fact that they
balance two entirely different notions of welfare: autonomy
and solidarity. Hence, they allow individuals the autonomy
to choose their preferred private goods whereas at the same
time welfare state provision of income and services enables
certain capabilities and functionings on the part of individuals from all sectors of the population. Outhwaite (2008) sees
the welfare state as a way for the state itself to survive. He
says that by becoming welfare states the morally bankrupt
national states found a way to survive after the Second World
War. It seems clear now, though, that increasing welfare is
less and less acceptable as a rationale for state activity and
expenditure and that the state is expected to find its legitimacy elsewhere.

Intermezzo

The next two chapters, comprising the third section of the book, are concerned with investigating how the arrangements for welfare actually operate in practice and the implications for people in everyday life. We seek as much as possible to situate the discussion at the level of the sociology of actors, with the aim of sketching an outline of how people go about securing welfare in affluent countries. The goal is more to apply our frame of thinking about welfare to particular domains of life than to identify hard and fast outcomes. This involves the formidable task of linking macro and micro, connecting formal arrangements for organising the distribution of resources and opportunities with how people organise themselves to obtain what is important to them in terms of material welfare. As outlined at the end of chapter 2, two meanings of welfare are developed. The first is material welfare, which relates to income but also material resources more broadly. The second sense of welfare is in terms of personal relationships and care. These are discussed more in chapter 6 (although the chapters should not be seen to operate a strict division between the two senses of welfare). Data shortages are the main factors imposing limits. In some parts we rely on income – given that it is the source of the most comparative and up-to-date data. While the limits of broad-based income data are recognised, they are nevertheless useful to indicate people's general circumstances. As much as possible, the chapters put income together with other factors, to paint a picture of a wider sense of welfare in terms of people's participation in a range of activities and relationships.

5

Securing Material Welfare through the Market and the State

This chapter seeks to identify the conditions and agency associated with securing material welfare, especially income, through the market and the state. In the first part, the focus is on the labour market. Conceived from the perspective of welfare, the labour market is a set of institutions and processes that act to include or marginalise and exclude. It seems especially important to examine the labour market warts and all, given the very idealistic terms in which it is portrayed in current political discourses. This section looks at the labour market critically from different angles but especially in respect of how different sectors of the population fare in employment. The second part of the chapter aims to get across how welfare state provisions affect people's levels of material welfare, especially from the perspective of income adequacy and inequality. The third section turns to income and inequality across social class groups and over the life course. The general investigative model that underlies the chapter is shown in box 5.1.

Welfare through Markets: Securing Welfare through Paid Work

Paid employment is the main way in which most people go about securing welfare. People's sources of income vary,

---

Box 5.1   Key elements of material welfare

Material welfare (income + employment participation opportunities) indicated by:

Labour market participation and income levels
Income inequality and poverty
Chances of mobility
Resources available through family, personal relations

---

though, within countries and across them. In regard to international comparisons, table 5.1 shows that in Germany salaries account for only about half of people's gross income compared with nearly 80 per cent in the US. Another great source of variation is how much transfers and benefits make up of people's income. On the basis of only a three-country comparison, as a proportion of gross income, this varies from nearly a third in Germany to only 13 per cent in the US. Straight away, then, it is obvious that welfare conceived of as income is derived from different sources in the three countries. This is partly to do with the organisation and operation of the labour market and partly also to do with the reach and nature of the welfare state.

The employment rate in the EU in 2009 was 64.6 per cent (Eurostat 2010a); in the US it was roughly similar.[1] This means that around a third of people of 'working age' (defined in the EU as between the ages of 15 and 64 years) are not

Table 5.1   Composition of Gross Income in Germany, UK and US (%), 2005

	Salary	Business	Property	Transfers
Germany	52	6	11	31
UK	69	8	4	20
US	79	6	2	13

Source: Calculated from www.worldsalaries.org (Table on Total Personal Average Income – International Comparison, available at: http://www.worldsalaries.org/total-personal-income.shtml).

involved in the labour market. Many of these are in education and a significant proportion are involved in providing care or are themselves ill or disabled in some way. Mainly for family and care-related reasons, the average employment rate for women is much lower than that for men – 58–60 per cent compared with 70–72 per cent for men. But female employment rates are going up or at least they were before the latest recession. The rise over the previous ten years was quite strong in some countries – in the EU as a whole some ten years ago just 52 per cent of working-age women were employed, so the average has risen by nearly 7 percentage points in the decade.[2] It is well known that patterns of male and female employment are closely tied to values and practices around family life. Change is, therefore, a complicated process of adjustment and negotiation and when women move into the labour market in large numbers they tend to develop employment patterns that are quite different to those of men (Daly 2000b). Overall though, women's participation in employment has been on an upward curve in Europe and the US, unlike the rates for men, which have been stable if not falling slightly (due to participation in education and unemployment).

There are various forms of exclusion from the labour market but 'unemployment' is the most commonly recognised official form. While the actual definition varies, unemployment is typically measured in terms of the numbers of people who present themselves as formally seeking and available for work. The unemployment rate in the EU as a whole for 2009 was 9 per cent (up from 6.7 per cent in March 2008) and in the US the rate was somewhat higher (at nearly 10 per cent). While the risk of unemployment has been elevated by the recent recession, unemployment is a fixture in the contemporary economic landscape. The long-term trend is for relatively high levels of unemployment in Europe anyway; since the 1980s unemployment in the EU has ranged somewhere between 8 and 10 per cent, for example. In the US it has varied more, with levels down to around 5 per cent at various times (as in the mid-2000s for example).

Unemployment has huge significance – both symbolic and in terms of material welfare – for people and also for societies, although the effects depend somewhat on how long it lasts.

Roughly about a third of those classified as unemployed in the EU in 2008 had been looking for work for at least a year – they were therefore officially considered as long-term unemployed (Eurostat 2010b: 64). Looked at from the perspective of individuals, one's chances of being unemployed are closely patterned by one's educational background. When measured between April and June 2009, for example, people in the EU with primary or lower secondary education as their highest level of educational achievement were almost three times (2.9) more likely to be unemployed as those who had completed university (ibid.: 75). This disparity, which exists in every country, has grown over time – in 2004 it was 2.4. The chances of unemployment are also patterned by age, with young people increasingly vulnerable – the unemployment rate for those aged between 15 and 24 years was 18.3 per cent in the EU in March 2009 (up from 14.7 per cent at the end of 2007) (Social Protection Committee 2009: 15). Nearly one in five of Europe's young people, then, is officially registered as unemployed.

There is also clustering of unemployment and worklessness: in 2007 close to one out of every ten adults aged between 18 and 59 years in the EU were living in a household where no one was working (Eurostat 2010b: 66). This phenomenon – so-called jobless households – has been problematised by the third way and other policy perspectives. The EU speaks now of 'household job intensity' to refer to the extent to which adult members of households make themselves available for employment (Social Protection Committee 2009). Apart from the fact that their incomes are lower and their risk of poverty very high, jobless households are seen to exemplify bad habits and act as a transmission belt for practices considered unacceptable. With targeted efforts to address it, in particular tying welfare benefits more closely to work participation or training, the proportion of jobless households across the EU is on the way down. However, since it is mainly people with intermediate levels of education who benefited from the increase in employment that took place during the 2000s, many in jobless households were left unaffected by the growth spurt given their lower levels of education (OECD 2008). As well as the already mentioned gender, age and educational differentiations, employment participation is typically lower for those with a disability, people from minority backgrounds and immigrants who are not EU citizens.

Being in paid work is not necessarily synonymous with welfare, however. Labour markets are highly differentiated and people's experience of paid work and the rewards they get from it vary hugely. One important indicator and constituent of this stratification is so-called earnings gaps – these refer to differences in earnings levels across different sectors of the employed. These are widespread and have been getting larger. Highly educated workers have been pulling further and further ahead in the pay stakes. The OECD (2008) estimates that the dispersion among male workers increased by around 10 per cent and by 11 per cent for women workers, between 1985 and 2005 with most of the rise occurring since 1995.[3] Wage inequalities have mainly been driven by increases at the upper end of the wage distribution rather than a collapse in wages at the bottom (ILO 2009a). So the already well-paid are paid more. This is not necessarily attributable to expertise – it is as much a value judgement as anything else. The recent economic crisis has revealed that those at the top level of companies and even of the public sector have managed to secure for themselves extremely high levels of remuneration, presumably through bargaining and self-promotion. But this, too, varies by country. The ratio of CEO compensation to the pay of production workers in manufacturing has been reported as 21:1 in Sweden, 31:1 in the UK and 41:1 in the US (Osberg and Smeeding [2006], cited in Wilkinson and Pickett 2009: 243). While it is difficult to predict how the recession will affect top earners, there is a good chance that they will continue to see huge increases and bonuses, although not as vast as in recent years. One other trend worthy of note is that the gap in the return for education has widened – although this effect is beginning to taper off (Brewer et al. 2009). Technology has played a key role: it has tended to complement the work of skilled and educated workers but substitute for that of lower-skilled workers. The latter, then, either become or remain low-waged or lose their jobs altogether.

Women generally can expect to do less well than men in employment, even though they are being employed in greater numbers. This relative disadvantage is true in many senses, but it is to be seen especially in terms of promotion, levels of seniority and pay. The last row in table 5.2 shows that nearly a third of women workers in three out of the four countries (Sweden being the exception) earned less than two-thirds of the male median wage in 2006. Gender gaps in wages have proved so resistant to measures to address them that they could be said to be a standard feature of contemporary labour markets. Across the EU countries in 2007, women were paid on average 17.5 per cent less than men, a differential which has remained stubborn and difficult to shift (Eurostat 2010b).[4] There is no model country in respect of gender gaps and such gaps cross the different types of welfare regime which were outlined in the last chapter. Yet it should also be noted that in all the eleven countries where the OECD investigated recent earnings dispersion (see n. 3), full-time working women at the lower end of the earnings distribution have recorded stronger growth in earnings as compared with low-earning, full-time working men. This suggests a shift in gender income dynamics in some families, although it is

Table 5.2   Indicators of financial well-being inequalities in Germany, Sweden, UK and US, 2006

	Germany	Sweden	UK	US
Ratio of income of top 20% to that of bottom 20%	4.1	3.5	5.4	—
Poverty among children under 16 (%)	12.0	14.0	24.0	—
Poverty among total population (%)	13.0	12.0	19.0	—
Low pay (% earning below 2/3 male median): Men	9.0	5.0	16.0	20.0
Women	31.0	9.0	29.0	29.0

Source: Created from tables 13.1 and 13.4, Stewart (2009).

not true of other groups of working women and men, and the experience overall is of relative female disadvantage in employment.

Looked at over time, the labour market is proving less and less safe and efficient as a source of income and financial security. This was the case even before the latest recession. Over time, a host of structural changes associated with globalising capitalism have rendered the jobs market less reliable in general, but especially for those who are in any way 'vulnerable'. While the details are too complex to discuss here, we can point to the major processes and some of the consequences.

One main process has been job shedding. Also known as 'downsizing', it involves a decision on the part of employers and companies to lay off staff, not necessarily because of a temporary drop in demand for a firm's products but to shed certain workers permanently so as to raise share prices, deal with competitive pressures or reorganise production processes (Hacker 2008: 68). A related process is that of job and plant relocation, as companies trawl the world for locations that yield the best returns, especially in terms of output and profits. This process is acted out throughout the affluent economies such that paid work is becoming scarcer and jobless growth a common phenomenon. Employment scarcity predated the recent economic crisis but it has also been worsened by it – the International Labour Organisation (ILO) estimates that the latest recession had cost over 20 million jobs by 2009 as well as putting many more at risk (ILO 2009b). The organisation also predicts that if participation rates fall by as little as 0.4 percentage points in the high GDP countries over the 2009–12 period, it would mean that some 12 million more people would be out of employment (ibid.: 8). The stalling of employment growth is also patterned, with certain categories of workers on the front line of the crisis. Youth are especially vulnerable – in the UK and the US the employment participation rates of young workers declined during 2008 and 2009 by around 2 and 4 percentage points respectively (ibid.). Other workers likely to be affected by job loss are the low-skilled, employees holding temporary contracts, mobile workers, migrants and older workers (Social Protection Committee 2009).

Changes in the types of available jobs and the nature of the employment relationship are also significant. In 2008 temporary work[5] comprised 14 per cent of total employment in EU countries and part-time work 18.2 per cent (Eurostat 2010b). While the proportion and distribution of these types of employment vary in different countries, they are closely associated with the rise of the service sector and in the industrialised countries as a whole have been growing as a proportion of total employment. Although service jobs are extremely diverse, major segments of the service sector – retail trade, the food industry, care-giving, customer relations – offer relatively low pay, restricted opportunities for advancement and little security (Hacker 2008: 81). The sector sweeps up large numbers of women workers, with part-time work being especially prevalent among women (accounting for 30.6 per cent of all female employment in the EU in 2008). Growth in non-standard employment is a long-term trend and it is one driven not necessarily by demand from women or other potential workers but rather by employers' efforts to cut labour costs and enhance productivity and flexibility. The situation has been worsened by the latest recession which has already induced a fall in average working hours – down 2.2 per cent in the most affluent countries – and an increase in the incidence of part-time work (ILO 2009b). People in these types of work situation also suffer a wage penalty. In the OECD countries, the equivalent hourly pay of part-time workers was about 25 per cent less than that for full-time workers in the mid-1990s, for example (OECD 2008: 83). It has been shown that this is not due to the characteristics of workers – in comparison to other workers so-called non-standard workers receive lower pay after controlling for differences in education and experience (Social Protection Committee 2009: 18). Across the EU, non-standard workers have a much higher risk of poverty than permanent and full-time workers (Eurostat 2010b: 50). It is also known that a significant proportion of part-time workers – 21.6 per cent in the EU in 2008 – would like to work longer hours. The proportion of such underemployed workers has grown – increasing threefold in the OECD area since 1985 (OECD 2008: 83).

All the evidence[6] suggests the existence of groups of workers who tend to remain at the margins of the labour market. Whether involved in part-time work or temporary contracts or unemployed, at least a quarter of the working-age population across Europe resembles a reserve army of labour. Young's interpretation (2007: 100) is that what he calls 'the lower class' is being reconstructed into a service class which provides services, servants and security for the rest of society. These are sometimes part of the formal economy but are often informal and below the radar, and sometimes illegal. Their experience of employment and unemployment operates to the convenience and demands of their employers and their conditions of work are very different and typically inferior to those pertaining in the employment mainstream. They include the seasonal farm workers, the entertainment industry workers and the army of drivers, domestics and security workers who keep life running smoothly for the majority of people. While they are most widespread in the big cities, they are to be found also in the small towns and villages. Young people, low-skilled women and men, migrants and people with an illness or disability all have high chances of being in this kind of marginalised employment situation. Looking across countries there is a predictability about those at the lowest rungs of the ladder – people with the same kinds of background appear again and again in the marginalised situations.

While they are not identical, this phenomenon of increasing marginalised employment is associated with a growing category of working poor, whom Jock Young (2007: 85) calls 'the over employed'.[7] In the EU as a whole in 2007, some 8 per cent of people in employment (aged 18 years and older) lived under the poverty threshold (Eurostat 2010b). The UK is close to the EU average in this but in the US the figures are much higher at over 10 per cent (OECD 2009). In most countries low wages are a cause of poverty. In the UK for example, recent evidence indicates that a tenth of employees earn less than £5.50 an hour and 30 per cent less than £7.50 (Hills et al. 2010).[8] The median hourly wage is £9.90. Significant in-work poverty levels suggest that some are not capable of warding off poverty by employment. They also serve to undo traditional distinctions between welfare and work (O'Connor 2001). A fundamental cause of poverty is the shift in policy from income support outside of employment to employment as the primary source of income for all. In the US, lifetime term limits on receiving social assistance have seen a massive movement of former benefit recipients into low-paid employment (Handler and Hasenfeld 2007: 320). Europe, too, has seen this kind of movement but on nothing like the scale of the US and with far more supportive policies in place (and transferring a far greater proportion of income to people, as we saw in table 5.1). There, too, things are changing, though: official reports from the EU now endorse 'high-intensity employment', by which is meant all adults in the household working more than part-time, as necessary to avoid low income, especially in households with children (Social Protection Committee 2009).

It is obvious, then, that the labour market has many 'leaky' aspects when viewed from the perspective of welfare. These act like funnelling mechanisms (see box 5.2). In sum, while the labour market provides financial security and well-being for many, it provides neither adequate income security nor opportunity for a significant subsection of the population. Moreover, there is a growing space between the rungs of the ladder.

Box 5.2   Examples of funnelling mechanisms in the labour market that limit welfare

Unemployment (affected by education and skill level but a function also of job shedding and company practices)
Low wages
Wage gaps (again based on education but also gender and ethnic background and whether one is able-bodied or not)
Part-time jobs
Informal work

Income Sources and Income Security

We have seen that wages have become increasingly polarised and that this is especially marked in the UK and the US. What about incomes in general? The top row of table 5.2 shows the income of the top fifth of income holders as a proportion of that of the bottom fifth. In the UK the top fifth have five times the income of the bottom fifth, in Germany the ratio is 4 and in Sweden it is 3.5. How does this happen and how is it changing?

For the main OECD countries taken as a whole, the distribution of household income became more unequal over the twenty years from the mid-1980s to the mid-2000s (OECD 2008: 26–7). The UK and the US figure prominently here again, the former especially. At risk of oversimplification: the income of the bottom fifth held constant in most countries, those in the middle-income bands generally lost ground (although not in the UK under New Labour), while those at the top were most commonly on an upward trajectory (a very sharp one in the US and UK). According to recent research in the UK, differences by social class or occupation are consistently the largest of any other factor considered (such as gender, age, level of disability, ethnic background, deprivation of area of residence) in affecting income and wealth levels (Hills et al. 2010: 252). Inequality was driven especially by very high salaries and bonuses for high earners as well as gains in income from stock options, capital gains, interest and dividends. These soared in the 1990s and 2000s while the returns to the great mass of wage earners contracted (Duménil and Lévy 2004). This is in stark contrast to what happened to incomes during the post-war boom period when income inequality was reduced and a far greater proportion of profits and high incomes was taxed.

Typically, in the western developed countries in the late 2000s the poorest half of the population have something between 20 and 25 per cent of all income and the richest half the remaining 75 or 80 per cent (Wilkinson and Pickett 2009: 17). Income inequality is on the increase – calculations for the OECD countries indicate that over the last twenty years income inequality as measured by the average change in the

Gini coefficient increased by 7 per cent (OECD 2008).[9] The recent report of the National Equality Panel in the UK suggests that on some measures income inequality in the UK is the highest it has been for the last fifty years (Hills et al. 2010). Inequality is also very high in the US. Within the EU, the UK is among the most unequal from the perspective of the distribution of income. For example, comparison of the share of all income held by the richest fifth with that of the poorest fifth put the UK as twelfth out of fifteen EU countries in terms of income inequality in 2006 (Hills et al. 2009: 343). Sweden stands out as a low income inequality country, although inequality is increasing there too. In fact, income inequality is growing almost everywhere, mainly because of gains at the top end of the income distribution (most typically because of income from investments and assets). One consequence is that middle-income families have lost ground – the so-called 'hollowing out of the middle class' (OECD 2008: 287). This took place especially in the US and the UK in the decade from the mid-1980s to the mid-1990s. From data available now anyway, it looks like New Labour policies shored up the position of the middle class within the income distribution in the UK (Hills et al. 2010).

There are indications also that insecurity in income is a rising problem. In the US, where long-term panel data is available on incomes, the data suggest that the instability of American families' incomes has risen faster than the inequality of families' incomes. As Hacker (2008: 27) puts it, while the gaps between the rungs of the ladder of the American economy have grown, what has increased even more quickly is how far people slip down the ladder when they lose their financial footing. The story he tells is of sky-rocketing instability in before-tax incomes among American families – income instability was higher in the 1980s as compared with the 1970s and higher again in the 1990s and, while it dropped during the boom of the late 1990s, it never fell below its starting level. 'Over the last generation, problems once confined to the working poor – lack of health insurance and access to guaranteed pensions, job insecurity and staggering personal debt, bankruptcy and home foreclosure – have crept up the income ladder to become an increasingly normal part of middle class life' (ibid.: xii).

While Europe does not appear to have the economic roller coaster that Hacker identifies for the US,[10] here too individuals and families have good and bad years, even good and bad decades. This is especially the case for those who are on moderate to low incomes. For example, a small study carried out in the UK of income patterns of ninety-three middle-income working families with children in the 2003–4 financial year found that only about a third had an income pattern that was stable (Hills et al. 2006). Moreover, a quarter of the families had highly erratic incomes. In fact, the study found that there were eight different types of income trajectory among the ninety-three families. The situation is likely to be even worse for those on low incomes. Research on these groups shows that unexpected expenses can be catastrophic but also that 'occasions', such as a marriage or a funeral and what are considered as 'normal' family transitions (such as the birth of a new baby or children moving into education), may be enough to push them across the poverty threshold (Daly and Leonard 2002; Lister 2004). But the force of change that Hacker is alluding to is a general exposure to a growing level of economic risk. This is acting to undermine both the labour market and the welfare state as sources of income security.

Duménil and Lévy (2004, 2009) are convinced that neo-liberalism is a class phenomenon, a new social order wherein the upper capitalist and managerial classes (the top 15 per cent or so) have triumphed in their ruthless search for ever higher incomes and greater freedom to appropriate the surpluses even if these surpluses are fictitious. Wealth and the wealthy are an integral part of this story. The latest *Wealth and Assets Survey* for the UK – providing a snapshot of the wealth distribution in the UK between 2006 and 2008 – reveals stark disparities (Office for National Statistics 2009a). The top 10 per cent of wealth-holders possess more than 44 per cent of all wealth. Wealth is more concentrated than income – the top 10 per cent of income earners receive 'only' 29 per cent of all income. Probing this further is insightful. While the Gini coefficient for income inequality is currently around 0.36 (a higher Gini coefficient signifies greater inequality), the Gini for total wealth in the UK is 0.61, for net property wealth it is 0.62 and for net financial wealth it is as high as 0.81.

Poverty

Increasing poverty is another part of the welfare landscape.[11] In the UK the figures for 2007–8 indicate that some 13.5 million people were below an income threshold of 60 per cent of the median household income (Brewer et al. 2009).[12] This figure, representing 22 per cent of the population, is an increase of some 1.5 million compared with three years previously (2004–5). When compared with other countries in Europe, the UK is a high-poverty country (see second and third rows of table 5.2). Of the western European countries, the UK's poverty prevalence most resembles the levels found in Ireland and the Mediterranean countries.

Poverty now affects the young more than the elderly. Children, and by implication the families in which they live, are especially vulnerable. In most countries children's risk of poverty is higher than that of adults (see table 5.2). A quarter of all children in the UK were living in households below the poverty line in 2006 compared with 14 per cent in Sweden and 12 per cent in Germany. Children outnumber adults in poverty in Sweden and the UK although not in Germany. In fact, there are only six countries in the EU where the poverty rate among children is lower than the adult rate: Cyprus, Denmark, Estonia, Germany, Finland and Slovenia (Eurostat 2010b). Children in the US are very vulnerable to poverty also. In 2004 the US child poverty rate was 29 per cent (Stewart 2009: 274). Among other things, this level of child poverty means that nearly half of all US children will have used food stamps at least once between the ages of 1 and 20, about a third will have used them for two or more years and 22.8 per cent for five or more years (Handler and Hasenfeld 2007: 90). Across countries, lone-parent households are very vulnerable to poverty, indeed to all forms of deprivation – in fact 40 per cent of the children in poverty in the UK live in such households. The child's risk of low income or poverty depends especially on the extent of employment among family members, but even when all family members are in employment there will still be a substantial group of children in poverty.

What difference does the welfare state make?

The Financial Achievements and Limitations of the Welfare State[13]

Social provision, says De Swaan (1988: 251), has levelled the peaks and depths of material existence. On average in twenty-four OECD countries in the mid-2000s, the average household got some 22 per cent of its disposable income from cash benefits (OECD 2008: 103). As has been indicated already, the level of state support varies widely across countries. In the US, for example, it was equivalent to 9.4 per cent of disposable income, in the UK 14.5 per cent, in Germany 28.2 per cent and in Sweden 32.7 per cent. The trend is actually downwards – since the mid-1990s benefits have fallen as a share of household income in a majority of these countries.

Not surprisingly, cash benefits are most important for those of retirement age – amounting on average to two-thirds of their income – whereas the average for people of working age is 15 per cent (ibid.). About a quarter of all public transfers in the main OECD countries go to the poorest fifth of households. But the 'progressivity' of welfare depends also on taxes – in general the combined contribution of public transfers and household taxes to those in the lowest income quintile is equivalent to around 4.2 per cent of disposable household income – it is 1.9 per cent in the US, 4.2 per cent and 4.1 per cent in Germany and the UK respectively and 5.7 per cent in Sweden (ibid.: 116). Cash benefits tend generally to effect greater redistribution than taxes.

Munzi and Smeeding (2008) show the overall impact by calculating the effects of taxes and transfers in alleviating income inequality and poverty. Using data from the Luxembourg Income Study for the period around 2000 for fifteen developed western nations, their results show that taxes and transfers customarily reduce inequality (measured by the Gini coefficient) in market incomes by about 32 per cent. Table 5.3 gives the percentage improvement effected in market income inequality and poverty rates for the four main countries of interest here. It shows major differences. Taking market income first, Sweden and Germany achieve a reduction in inequality in excess of 40 per cent. Of the countries included in their analysis – the major European countries as

Table 5.3 Reduction in income inequality in market income and poverty (%) *c.* 2000

	Market income	Poverty rate
Germany	41	70
Sweden	44	77
UK	31	61
US	21	26

Source: Munzi and Smeeding (2008: 52–3), calculated from figures 2.3 and 2.4.

well as Australia, Canada and the US – the latter has the highest level of inequality in net disposable income and its system of taxation and benefits effects least reduction in inequality (only 21 per cent). The UK is between the two extremes at 31 per cent. Countries do better on poverty reduction, effecting an average decrease of 61 per cent in poverty when measured on the basis of market income (that is, prior to transfers). Reading the two sets of statistics together indicates that transfer and tax systems tend to redistribute more income to the lower-income sectors than they take away income from the high-income sectors of the population. Of the countries considered here, Sweden effects by far the greatest decrease in poverty (some 77 per cent), followed by Germany at 70 per cent. Once again the US is at the bottom – making the least anti-poverty effort of any nation (26.4 per cent). The UK effects around an average reduction in poverty (at 61 per cent).

Overall, the fifteen nations can be compressed into two main groupings on the basis of the volume of redistribution effected by their tax and transfer systems. The Anglo-Saxon (including the UK, Ireland and the US) and southern European countries belong to the worst half of the ranking in terms of both the prevalence of poverty and the reduction in poverty effected by taxes and transfers and the northern European and Scandinavian nations are in the better half. Lest we jump to simplistic assumptions, however, Munzi and Smeeding point out that there is no one kind of programme or set of programmes that is conspicuously successful in all countries (ibid.: 60–1). The US is distinct from all the other countries, though, in its emphasis on employment and self-reliance for working-age adults, regardless of the wages that workers must accept or the family situation of workers. In that country, it is the strong economy of the 1990s which produced the greatest anti-poverty effect. This bodes ill for the intervening period and especially since 2008, which among other things has seen unemployment soar and what looks like a permanent haemorrhaging of jobs.

What proportion goes to the lowest income sectors? In the UK 57 per cent of cash benefits go to the bottom 40 per cent of people (Office for National Statistics 2009b). An important point to note, though, is that a lot of the redistribution is not vertical (from rich to poor) but horizontal – from young to old, from those who work to those who do not, and from the childless to families with children (Förster and Pearson [2002], cited in Byrne 2005: 96).

Inequality and Opportunity

Conceptions of welfare embrace the idea of progression in social and socio-economic terms whereby people can improve their situation vis-à-vis that of their parents. Widespread social mobility has been the norm in post-war European societies whereby large sectors of the population equal or better their parents' socio-economic status (Erickson and Goldthorpe 1992; Breen 2004). This does not appear to be any longer the case and it certainly cannot be taken for granted for the future.

Data comparing intergenerational earnings for the cohorts born in 1958 and 1970 in Britain suggest that the earnings of those born in 1970 were more closely related to the income of their parents as compared with those born in 1958 (Blanden and Machin 2008). That is, fewer people are moving away from their originating position (interpreted in terms of the income level of their parents). Other evidence also suggests decreasing chances of upward mobility. For example, the gap in obtaining a university degree between children born in the fifth richest and poorest families widened for those born in 1970 as compared with the earlier generation. The evidence on intergenerational change can be interpreted as pointing to a fall in relative income mobility between generations (Blanden et al. 2005). However, some sociologists dispute this and suggest that if one takes social class mobility as one's marker there is really no change in the level of social mobility (Goldthorpe and Jackson 2007). There are also suggestions that the policies pursued by the New Labour governments from 1997 to 2010 might lead to some improvements and that access to education was unquestionably more equal in 2008 than in 1997 (Lupton et al. 2009). Certainly, the numbers of young people from poor backgrounds staying on at school have improved although huge gaps still exist between the educational access, performance and attainment of children from well-off and poor backgrounds (ibid.). One thing is clear overall: in Europe and the US social mobility seems to have plateaued out and is not increasing as it did in the post-war period.

Inequality affects not just individuals but also society itself. The argument by Wilkinson (1996) and Wilkinson and Pickett (2009) – to the effect that inequality is itself causal to a whole series of deleterious welfare-related outcomes such as poor health – is one of the strongest formulations of the relationship. In the view of these authors, inequality decreases social cohesion or, put otherwise, egalitarian societies have higher levels of social cohesion than inegalitarian societies. The idea is that egalitarian societies have strong community bonds between people, more involvement in social and voluntary activities outside the home and less antisocial aggressiveness and stress and anxiety. The specificities of the thesis are disputed – the causal mechanisms are the subject of particular scepticism (Jencks 2002). In any case, as Orton and Rowlingson (2007: 63) point out, a less ambitious thesis may be sustained in that a review of the evidence on the effects of inequality on a range of socio-economic factors does underline inequality as a problem. The scale of income differences in a society is revealing about the social hierarchy in place. The scale of material inequalities provides the skeleton or framework around which class and cultural differences are formed (Wilkinson and Pickett 2009: 28). Over time differences in occupational position gradually become overlaid by differences in clothing, aesthetic taste, education, sense of self and a range of other markers of identity (ibid.; Devine et al.

2005). The underlying process is depicted as a movement of stratification from the material to the cultural and from collective inequality to individualised inequalities. 'Post-class societies remain differentiated, unequal and conflictual, but along shifting and unpredictable lines' (Outhwaite 2008: 110).

Wilkinson and Pickett's underlying point is of a change in the social order itself. Byrne (2005: 81) speaks of 'a phase shift' in the character of contemporary capitalism, a polarised form of postindustrial capitalism. Associated with this is a phase shift in income distribution and inequality. Duménil and Lévy (2009), too, see a new social order. This is capitalist and class-based whereby the last three decades have not just vastly increased the returns to capital but they have channelled the gains more and more to a relatively small sector of the population located towards the top of the income spectrum. So the deregulation and other forms of support from governments for globalised economic activity, the relentless pursuit of returns to shareholders and investments, the encouragement of high consumer debt and cuts in taxes and benefits have been of limited benefit to the population at large and have seriously disadvantaged the lower-income sectors. There are different ways of depicting the kind of society that this leads to. Some have suggested that we should view today's society as based on inequality. Hutton (1995) speaks of a 30/30/40 society whereby there is a bottom 30 per cent of unemployed and economically inactive people who are to all intents and purposes marginalised. Another 30 per cent, while in paid work, are in forms of employment that are structurally insecure. This leaves 40 per cent of people who hold jobs that can be seen as secure and identity confirming.

Life Courses and Trajectories

One way of pinning the changes to individuals' lives is to think in terms of a trajectory or pattern established over time through a life-course perspective. Welfare states, viewed not just in terms of their income supports but also in terms of the different services that they provide such as health, education and housing, make a major contribution to structuring people's lives by helping to demarcate specific temporal structures of life. They do this through their definitions of and support for events, phases, episodes and transitions (Leisering and Walker 1998; Leisering and Leibfried 1999). The labour market has a key role here as well and in fact it is the interaction between the state and the labour market that is so influential. First, they both help to frame the very definition of stages of life (e.g. childhood, adulthood, old age); second, they influence the connections between these three standard phases of life and smoothe the transition between phases; third, they affect the course of people's lives by reinforcing particular normative models about appropriate behaviour. A life-course perspective is helpful in recognising not just the regularity of life phases but the connections among the different phases of life. Karl Ulrich Mayer (1986) is very clear that life course is associated with causal processes around inequality. According to him, the perspective is especially useful for revealing trajectories and transitions and demonstrating how these constitute organised and patterned sets of progression that involve particular sets of experience (and presumably outcomes). While our understanding is still at the early stages – not least because data tracing incomes over time is scarce – we do know something about particular groups and transitions that is insightful in the context of the present discussion.

These effects extend quite widely. We know that for people born in 1970 in the UK growing up poor doubled their chances of being poor as an adult, and for those born in the 1980s the odds had quadrupled (Blanden and Gibbons 2006). There are two main findings here: intergenerational poverty persistence has doubled; there is especially a persistence of poverty from the teens into adulthood. So among these two generations, people born into poor families were less likely to break free of their background and fulfil their potential as compared with earlier generations born into similar circumstances. For teenagers growing up in the 1970s in the UK it was family characteristics (for example, poor educational level of parents, low parental employment rates) that mainly accounted for their poverty, whereas for those who were teenagers in the 1980s it was poverty itself that put them at a significant disadvantage (ibid.). This links into two more general concerns and findings. First, there is greater polarisation among younger cohorts between those who do well and those who do not as compared with, say, twenty years ago. Secondly, young adults entering the labour market in the 1980s and since, especially in the US, have not done as well as earlier cohorts, although they are better educated. For Hacker this is evidence of the existence of a ceiling on the returns to education for workers in the US (2008: 74). Education, he says, is not a risk-free investment.

It would be wrong to see things in static terms. People's situation does change and individuals and households experience economic cycles. This is the breaking news in regard to poverty anyway. Research on the dynamics of poverty in the UK indicates that only about 4 per cent of all households are persistently in the poorest fifth of households and about 12 per cent – some 10 million people – are in the poorest fifth of households at least two years out of three.[14] In the US poverty is more persistent, with 7 per cent of households in poverty for at least three years (OECD 2008: 158).[15]

Poverty exerts a kind of 'dragging effect', though. Several studies show that the probability of exiting poverty falls rapidly after having been poor for two or more years (Bane and Ellwood 1986). Entry into poverty mainly reflects family- and job-related events (OECD 2008). Family events (such as divorce, widowhood or childbirth, for example) are very important as causes of poverty – in fact, across OECD countries changes in family structure have been identified as the most important trigger of entry into poverty (ibid.: 167). Fully a quarter of poverty spells in the US, for example, begin with the birth of a child (Hacker 2008: 101). By comparison, a fall in the number of workers in a household accounts for far fewer entries into poverty – this plus a reduction of transfer income is more important for poverty entry among those who are poor in two consecutive years (OECD 2008: 168). Conversely, getting married and finding a job increases the probability of moving out of poverty.

There is no singular reading of the information on poverty dynamics, however. Policy makers like to interpret it positively – deducing that poverty is not an entrenched feature of most people's lives. However, by implication the other side of the variability of poverty thesis is that poverty reaches wider in society, affecting many more people at some point in their lives than was commonly believed. Jacob Hacker has calculated that a child poverty rate of 20 per cent in the US means that more than half of all American children will have spent at least a year in poverty by the time they reach 18 years of age (2008: 32). There is also the fact that people do not move very far, and to say that they 'exit' poverty is deceptive because the vast majority of those in poverty in one year are found to have moved only marginally if at all by the third year (OECD 2008: 171). Change is not simply a matter of crossing a threshold therefore. It also seems that measurement error may lead to overestimations of poverty dynamics. Using a modelling strategy that reduces bias and corrects for error, Worts et al. (2010) find that between 1993 and 2003 poverty in Britain and the US was more stable and less widely dispersed than previously assumed.

Overview

In this chapter we have considered how people fare in the labour market and the role of that set of institutions as well as those of the welfare state in giving people an adequate income, redistributing income more equally and structuring people's life courses in a more egalitarian manner. While they significantly change and improve the lives of many, both the labour market and the welfare state have strong sets of hierarchical mechanisms which lead to inequalities in the levels of material welfare obtained by different sectors of the population. There is a significant subset of people for whom welfare is a story of risk, insecurity and under-provision. We have seen that similar groups of people are at risk across countries – these include especially those with low or no skills, those with significant experience and risk of unemployment (which include many of the former but also others such as lone mothers, people with a disability or illness) and those from ethnic minority backgrounds. We have identified factors that act as funnelling mechanisms – such as low pay, temporary contracts, part time work even – which have the effect of reducing the welfare achievable by people from paid labour.

It is the case that, counter to much of the received wisdom of the third way and neo-liberal philosophies, participation in paid employment carries no welfare-related guarantees. Indeed, just at the time when the market is being promoted more and more as a source of welfare, it is delivering less. OECD data suggest that, on average, people living in households with workers account for around 60 per cent of the income-poor (OECD 2008: 134). The developments in the US especially show that the promises of the labour market often ring hollow. In the tentative recovery from the latest recession, for example, job creation has been especially sluggish and the recovery of profits for corporations has far outstripped job recovery (Sum and McLaughlin 2010). It has become a recession for workers rather than for corporations – the recovery in the US thus far has seen the most lopsided gains ever in corporate profits relative to real wages and salaries in that country's history (ibid.: 3). These patterns have not come out of nowhere. Before 1990, it took an average of 21 months for the US economy to regain the jobs shed during a recession; by 1990 and 2001 the time period had increased to 31 and 46 months respectively (Goodman 2010). The latest one now appears increasingly like a jobless recovery.

The welfare state, too, has a major function in equalising resources and opportunity structures, but this is one of a number of its elements and so it, too, is far from a universal guarantor of welfare. Poverty rates have been increasing. Between the mid-1980s and mid-2000s the poverty rate jumped by 13 per cent on average across the twenty-four countries for which data are available (OECD 2008: 129). On top of this, income inequality levels remain at their highest level for decades. When one puts it all together and locates the changes in a temporal pattern, it is clear that the last neo-liberal decades – especially the 1990s and 2000s – shifted the structure of advantage decisively in favour of those located towards the top of the income pyramid. This is true almost everywhere but the U-turn on inequality was especially characteristic of the Anglo-Saxon countries – the UK, US, Canada, Australia and New Zealand (Therborn 2009).

6

The Personal and Social Relations of Welfare

This chapter takes forward two issues running throughout the text: the intent to broaden the conception of welfare beyond the material and to demonstrate that welfare-generating activity is to be found also in the 'informal sphere' of family and community. Welfare theorising, says Smith (1993: 245), often isolates the individual or family unit. We must therefore recognise the family as a crucial arrangement for welfare, as much a part of societal organisation as the economy or the state. In its first part, the chapter devotes attention to the idea of the family and household as a resource unit, a sphere of redistribution of material and immaterial resources and also a source of other welfare-generating activities. One line of analysis focuses on income and assets and how these are 'redistributed' on a familial basis, another focuses on 'family solidarity' (in the sense of norms about family members helping each other), and another on care-giving and -receiving. At the root of the chapter are questions about what people give and get back in family life and how this might or might not be welfare conferring. These can only be treated in a rather sketchy fashion, however, mainly because of information shortages. We know little about how families operate in practice. The chapter then broadens out the analysis to consider in turn how welfare states seek to affect family-based welfare and how welfare is located in and generated by community-based activities, considering in turn some indicators of family policy orientation, welfare activity in the community and voluntary sectors and how embeddedness in local relations is welfare-enhancing. We also look at general trends around social support and trust and the extent to which people feel socially integrated in their communities and society more broadly. These, too, are only treated in brief, mainly because of space constraints.

There is a set of theoretical points to be made at the outset. To be properly understood, welfare needs to be conceptualised from a family or household perspective because welfare is a relation: what it means and how it is practised rely crucially on other people and other activities. Welfare cannot be achieved independently of others. Further, for the purposes of this chapter, family is seen more in terms of a set of relationships than a particular location or structure. In thinking through the relational aspects of welfare from a sociological perspective, it is helpful to differentiate between the household as a primarily economic unit and the family as a primarily social and sociological entity. A household is a living arrangement or pattern that smacks of function and utility; a family, on the other hand, is one of a small number of primary social institutions characterised by emotion and affect and embedded in kinship-based norms and relations. Of course, the family can be looked at economically – its activities relate in key ways to income redistribution, labour supply and consumption. This is the stuff of part of this chapter. But the family has to be looked at more broadly, more sociologically also. Through this lens, the family is a form of social organisation that provides for care needs, arranges intergenerational and gender relations and through these and other means plays a key part in individual and collective welfare. Although in this chapter we use the definite article (*the* family), it is not meant to refer to a particular kind of family or to imply that family life and organisation are homogeneous. Indeed, the entire chapter is intended to convey the message that families need to be conceived of as complex, multilayered and diverse. It is recognised from the outset, therefore, that one should speak of families rather than 'the' family.

It should be pointed out that the absence of other locations and forms of productive activity apart from the economy has

Table 6.1   Family and material and relational welfare

	Redistribution	'Production'
Material	Sharing of income and other resources Inheritance of property, income and assets	Household services
Relational	Family culture as capital Passing on of knowledge and contacts	Care and other forms of social and emotional support

been a major point of criticism about how national-level welfare activity is measured. This criticism is levelled especially at the GDP as a measure.[1] Feminists among others decried the missing contribution of the household and of non-market goods and services to welfare (Waring 1988). Analytically, there are a number of different levels at which households and especially families can be considered as conferring welfare (table 6.1). Differentiating between resource redistribution and welfare production and between welfare as material and relational helps for clarification purposes.

Family and Resource Distribution

First, the family or household is a location of income redistribution. Although much of the detail of intra-familial transfers is unknown, there are different ways in which the family is, hypothetically anyway, a conduit of resources. At the most basic level, living with others reduces one's risk of poverty and low income because of economies of scale associated with sharing fixed and other costs among more than one person. If four people use the same living space, the costs are less than if the space is shared by only two people. This is one of the reasons why family breakdown is so threatening. Roberts ([2004], cited in Handler and Hasenfeld 2007: 287) calculates for the US that if a couple with one child separates into one two-person unit and one single-person unit they would need an extra 40 per cent on top of their original income to avoid poverty. The act of setting up two households from one involves a whole set of additional costs.

However, we do not know the extent to which families actually function as distributors of resources. This must be highlighted at this early stage as a major information gap. The studies from which most information on income and its distribution is derived tend to stop at the front door (Folbre 1986). Such studies focus mostly on individual income or household income and they assume that income pooling is universal and unproblematic. Hence, collective income tends to be calculated on the basis of assumed perfect pooling and equal sharing among adults and among adults and children. To the extent that 'sharing' of resources within families has been examined empirically, it has been the subject of small-scale and micro-level studies, which ask people about how they budget and spend their income (e.g. Pahl 1989; Daly and Leonard 2002). This research paints a picture of variation in how money is managed and shared within families. Pahl (1989), for example, found four different systems, varying in terms of which partner had control and whether and to what extent the income was pooled or kept separate. Until we know more about how income is distributed within families, much about family as an institution of welfare is hidden from us.

There is another sense also in which the family can potentially aid distribution. A large body of evidence suggests that people engage in 'income stretching' and that much of this takes place within the context of family. As Walker and Collins (2004) point out, a low income means that families have little choice but to plan budgets meticulously: setting priorities, storing money for later, making lists even before wages or benefits are collected, tallying up the bill as they shop, and shopping frequently to avoid supplies at home being raided prematurely (see also Kempson et al. 1994). It is women who typically take on such activities. The endeavour of managing money is quite specialised. For example, people cut back on luxuries and leisure, shop in discount stores, visit markets for end-of-the-day sell-offs, scour the neighbourhood for bargains, and negotiate the trade-off between price and quality, especially in the case of clothing (Walker and Collins 2004: 205–6). Budgeting takes time, know-how, and patience. Food, although a priority expenditure, is often used to manage cash flows: food purchases have to fit in with the payment of important bills, notably the rent and services such as electricity (Daly and Leonard 2002).

A somewhat different way of approaching the matter of the nature of the relationship between family and welfare is through the concept of family solidarity. This, a normative concept with some origins in the analysis of kinship ties, helps to differentiate between on the one hand material, instrumental mutual aid (from monetary exchanges to the provision of services) and on the other social ties and inclusion in relational networks (Martin 2004: 3–4). It has been said that family cultures offer resources to deal with problems and opportunities (Saraceno 2008: 48). While the idea of family culture is immaterial, there is also a material side to the idea of family solidarity. Research indicates that transfers between generations play an important role in all advanced societies (Saraceno et al. 2005; Blome et al. 2009). Kohli (1999), in an investigation of transfers between generations in Germany, France and the US, found that their extent was considerable, although varying cross-nationally. Some 64 per cent of French parents had made financial transfers to their children in the past five years, as had 29 per cent of German parents and a quarter of American parents. In the UK, the evidence suggests that family transfers, especially through inheritance, are an increasing factor in both living standards and inequality. For instance, by 2005, nearly half of young first-time house buyers had benefited from assistance from family or friends with their deposit for their house or apartment. This is shot through with social class differentiations, however. Those receiving such assistance were able to pay deposits of £34,000, compared to only £7,000 for others (Hills et al. 2010: 380). Similarly, the chances of receiving an inheritance are highly correlated with people's existing wealth – the already wealthiest are most likely to receive the highest bequests.

A further type of resource transferred through families is immaterial in nature – it refers to social contacts and networks as well as cultural resources as forms of capital.

There are different elements to this. The rise and rise of social capital as a focus of sociological and other research endeavour has drawn attention to family as a source and conduit of cultural resources (Furstenberg and Kaplan 2004). The strong instrumentalist seam in this scholarship treats families as a site of social capital generation; family is thereby seen to generate a set of resources that are passed on and can be used outside the family. An underlying point is that family inheritance is much broader than money or material assets. Lareau's (2003) study into class-related differences as regards approaches to child-rearing in the US suggests, for example, that not just family background but social class factors are woven into the texture and rhythms of daily family life. She identifies a varying approach or 'cultural logic' among parents from different socio-economic backgrounds. The details may be familiar. Middle- or upper-class parents engage in what she calls 'concerted cultivation', actively fostering and continually assessing their children's talents, capabilities and skills. They enrol their children in numerous age-specific, organised activities and generally work hard to ensure that their children possess the appropriate class attributes. Parents, mothers especially, become *de facto* chauffeurs, shuttling their children from one set of life- and cognitive-enhancing activities to another. The child-rearing approach of the working-class and poor parents in Lareau's study emphasises, by contrast, the 'accomplishment of natural growth'. These parents view children's development as unfolding naturally as long as they are provided with comfort, food, shelter and other basic support. So children from the upper socio-economic groups are consciously groomed and fitted out for life, taught to develop an individualised sense of self, whereas children from working-class backgrounds are much more reliant on their own natural capacities and endowments and what is available to them locally.

Living a childhood in low income and poverty is known to be associated with a host of present and future consequences and costs. The costs visit children themselves, their families, communities and societies and include poor educational outcomes, lower future employment prospects, poor health and development, poorer family relationships and increased chances of becoming involved in crime and negative behaviours (Griggs and Walker 2008). The effects start very young. For example, children entering primary school in the UK in 2005–6 whose mothers had university degrees were assessed as being six months developmentally ahead of children whose mothers had no qualification above Grade D at GCSE (Hills et al. 2010). In fact, every extra £100 in monthly parental income when children are young is associated with a difference equivalent to a month's child development.

Welfare, as we have seen in chapter 2, is intimately related to personal relations, and family is central here also. Family networks are known to play an important role in social integration although this is difficult to measure. Information from the European Quality of Life Survey (first carried out in 2003 and repeated in 2007) reveals four key things about family support in Europe. First, such support is widespread. For example, over 70 per cent of people in the EU countries listed a family member as their first choice if they needed €1,000 to deal with an emergency. If feeling depressed, 65 per cent said they would turn first to a family member (Anderson et al. 2009). This conveys a sense of the family as active in personal support. Secondly, family life emerges as the most satisfying life domain across countries, but especially in the EU15 (Böhnke 2005: 27). People selected family first over accommodation, health, job, standard of living, social life and education as the aspect of their lives which was the source of greatest satisfaction. Third, the unemployed and under-employed and lone parents in Europe would be otherwise at risk of social isolation were it not for family networks (Saraceno et al. 2005: 108). Böhnke (2008a) shows that poor people living in shared households, with large families or with children, have a better chance of being socially integrated as compared with those in other types of living situation. In addition, it tends to be people from middle- and low-education backgrounds who are more family-centred (in the sense of the importance of the family as a source of support and relationships). Fourth, those embedded in family relations are less likely to experience feelings of isolation. In the EU countries – where satisfaction with life is generally very high – satisfaction with family life is the strongest determinant of subjective quality of life (Delhey 2004).

Family as Location of Welfare Production

A second relevant aspect of family is the production and consumption of goods and services. When viewed as an economic unit, the family is a major producer of goods for consumption (e.g. meals, laundry, personal care). This is to all intents and purposes unmeasured, however; household production (loosely, the work that goes on within the household) is typically excluded from the formal measures of economic activity in the national accounts. Some efforts have been made to value the activities involved, though, many of them by feminist scholars.[2] When the Office for National Statistics in the UK calculated estimates on an experimental basis in 2002, the results suggested that the value added to the economy by UK households in 2000 was some £695 billion (equivalent to 78 per cent of GDP as defined by the national accounts excluding household product) (Allin 2007: 50). Ringen concludes that half of the economy in Britain is a family economy: 'Society sits on a capital of family enterprise' (Ringen 2007: 159). The matter of how this 'capital' is put together and redistributed is not entirely straightforward, however. The issue of sharing again comes up. It is especially likely to be tricky in the context of the family where sharing is mediated by sets of relations and normative obligations. Equal sharing is assumed to be the case by the researchers even if not all members contribute an equal share of family income. Operating on the assumption that such complementarity prevails, my own work on income and poverty in Germany and the UK suggests that the family or household is the site of considerable income redistribution but that this is heavily gendered (Daly 2000a). Married women in Germany rely on their spouses to provide some 64 per cent of their economic resources and British women some 43 per cent (ibid.: 191).

The welfare-conferring contribution of the family also resides in the activities or tasks that it is involved in. A classic line of development in sociology focused on the social functions performed by families. Talcott Parsons (with Bales 1955), one of the leading members of the structural functionalist school of sociology, attributed to the family, in the context of greater family specialisation, key tasks associated with child socialisation and stabilisation of adult personality. Nobel prize winner Gary Becker (1981), too, theorised the family in terms of specialisation but in his case it was economic specialisation.[3] There is much talk of the family being stripped of its traditional functions. An influential line of argument is that economic development and technological change made it more efficient to locate some services that were formerly based in the family outside of it (Becker 1981). Child and elderly care and education are among the functions argued to have been transferred in part if not in whole to external forms of organisation. In some ways this argument dovetails with that of more recent sociology theorising of increasing individualisation of social life. Influential sociological theories (Beck 1992; Beck and Beck-Gernsheim 1995) depict a trend towards de-traditionalisation and individualisation. As a consequence, pre-given life-trajectories are said to be declining in import as people's life choices and biographies become increasingly personalised. The institutions of marriage and kinship are said to be weakened and family becomes a matter more of choice than of need.

Both types of claim have been contested, however. There is no doubt that forms of family life have changed and that one must speak of 'families' rather than 'family' and that when one does so one is referring to very different types of family. There is no doubt either but that internal family relationships have changed, focusing more on affection, emotion and relationship quality. In addition, the evidence suggests that families are more than ever before child-centred, emotionally and also in terms of how parents spend their time and resources. It seems that parents are investing more time in their children (Bianchi et al. 2006). This is true especially of well-educated parents – emerging work from the US indicates that there is an education gradient in parental time spent with children such that higher-educated parents even though they work more hours in the labour market spend more time on childcare than those with lower education (Hurst et al. 2008). Indeed, it seems that for higher-income parents childcare has eaten into the time devoted to household activities such as cleaning and cooking and even 'leisure'. Time with children is, then, more highly valued than ever. Observed originally in the US, the pattern has also been found in a number of other countries whereby time spent with one's children is more highly valued by those who have higher demands on their time. Greater parental time investment in children should not be taken to imply that people's time investment in other areas of family life is insignificant. It is not. Men and women of working age in Europe spend between two and four hours a day, respectively, on domestic work (Aliaga 2006). This includes significant amounts of time devoted to food preparation and cleaning and other household tasks.

Overall then, while the increasing room for choice and the de-traditionalisation of some institutions have been generally accepted, the theories of decline in the significance of family can be criticised as an unwarranted generalised abstraction from particular instances (Therborn 2004). Such claims also deny family any real agency, seeing change as being imposed from outside rather than treating families as active in changing their own situation and as agents of social change more generally.

It is possible to demonstrate empirically that families are heavily involved in care-related provision.

First, in most countries, families are still the major providers of care. While the evidence base tends to be somewhat unreliable and some countries are marked by significant differences in practices around care of the elderly as against that for children, nevertheless the indications are that families continue to be the major provider of care in most countries (with the Scandinavian nations as the exceptions). Table 6.2 presents some data comparing the situation across three of our four countries on the extent of the family's involvement in the care of children.

The data give pause for thought about the extent to which family is being divested of its activities, in relation to childcare anyway. Family is clearly foremost as a provider of such care. However, there is variation across the three countries. Families have the strongest childcare role in the UK, providing the mainstay, some 80 per cent, of childcare. Germany is the next closest – family care accounts for 70 per cent of all childcare there. One point of interest is that family care is broad-based, especially in the UK and Germany where grandparents play an important role. This kind of finding, together with other

Table 6.2   Care provision for children by families, 2004/5

	Germany	Sweden	UK
% of childcare provided by parent at home	32.9	24.5	42.1
% provided by family member other than parent (mainly grandparents)	27.5	2.8	25.3
Total % of care provided by family	70.0	28.5	80.9

Source: Adapted from Bahle (2009: 38), table 1.3 – note that the data refer to the main forms of current childcare arrangements for families with children under 12 years at the time of survey (data from European Social Survey, late 2004 and early 2005).

evidence, suggests that viewing family as coterminous with the nuclear family arrangement is erroneous. It is not the classic nuclear family care in the sense of parental care but rather a mix which includes grandparents, other relatives and parents. From the data above, only for Sweden is it possible to talk of a defamilisation of care of young children or indeed socialisation of family functions. Sweden is exceptional, though, and for Europe as a whole reference to defamilisation of childcare is not appropriate as a description of what has happened. It seems that out of home provision is a supplement to rather than a replacement for family care.

However, welfare in a family context is now especially conceived in terms of fathers' involvement in family life and the lives of children in particular. Empirical data suggest that change in male behaviour is slow, although in some countries such as the US men's involvement in the care of their children has grown substantially in the last decade or so (Hook 2006). Men still 'prioritise' paid work, though, while women not only put in longer hours overall but engage in a combination of paid and unpaid work, with strong overlaps in the type of activity that they actually do in both spheres. One could put it like this: sometimes women are paid for what they do and sometimes not.

Care of the elderly presents a generally similar picture. A survey in the EU in 2003 found that 5 per cent of the sample engage in such care on a daily basis and another 5 per cent at least once a week (Saraceno 2008: 62). In the UK estimates suggest that some 12 per cent of the adult population – almost 6 million people – provide unpaid care for elderly people on a regular basis (Carers UK 2007). Care-giving is very widespread among those still of working age. For example, among respondents involved in the first wave of the British Household Panel Survey in 1991, over half (51.8 per cent) of those still of working age in 2001 participated in informal care during at least one of the years between 1991 and 2001 (as reported in Carmichael et al. 2008). The peak age for becoming an informal carer is between 45 and 64 years in the UK, and around 45 per cent of carers fall into this age bracket. But it is also important to note that some 1 per cent of carers are children (aged between 5 and 15 years) and 5 per cent are people aged 85 or older. The majority of informal carers, approximately 60 per cent, are women. This pattern of care as a predominantly female activity is more or less universal across countries. There have been numerous attempts to calculate the value of the care provided in economic terms. In the UK, for example, it has been estimated that the value of care provided to the elderly in the context of family, neighbourliness and friendship is in the region of £87 billion annually, more than the annual costs of all aspects of the National Health Service in the year for which the calculation was made (2006/7) (Carers UK 2007).

All of the discussion thus far has had a particular slant, mining family life for its benefits. There are two dangers here: that we adopt a utilitarian approach, and that we represent family only as a source of welfare (as against diswelfare). In regard to the former, it needs to be pointed out that family relations are not just or even functional but are, rather, based on emotion and affect and embedded in systems of meaning that have a cultural base. As such family relations involve exchanges and reciprocities that are not primarily interpretable in an instrumental idiom. Insights such as these come from a number of sources. As we saw in chapter 2, the literature on care-giving and -receiving, for example, emphasises the uniqueness and complexity of care; that it has to be seen as a relationship, a set of activities, and an orientation or way of being. Care has been developed as a moral perspective or orientation, an ethical practice, requiring from the care-giver attentiveness, responsibility, competence and responsiveness (Tronto 1993; Held 2005). This means that there are elements of family relationships that can never be known, not to mind quantified. The critique extends into economics as well. Feminist scholars have posited the notion of the 'other economy' (Donath 2000). This has a number of distinctive features. In contradistinction to the production of commodities, it is concerned with the direct production and maintenance of human beings as an end in itself. Secondly, it functions by gift and reciprocity rather than by 'exchange'. This means that it refrains from and indeed objects to putting a monetary or instrumental value on and seeing family-based relationships in instrumental terms.

The second qualification relates to the charge of treating family only as welfare conferring. There are a number of risks associated with viewing family only in positive terms. For example, we know that family is a location of power and that to treat family in a unitary fashion flies in the face of knowledge about inequalities among family members. Children are an obvious example of family members who may lack power, influence and own resources within families. Women, too, are known to have less power especially if power derives from income procurement. The family is also a known site of violence. It is for these kinds of reason that there are major reservations to be lodged about the accuracy of household income and its intra-household redistribution when measurement takes little account of individual differences in access to resources within households or families (Burton et al. 2007). Families can also be instrumental in resisting change. While inequalities and resistance to change are not automatically sources of diswelfare, families are conservative institutions in many ways.

How do welfare states interact with and seek to affect families as welfare generating?

Welfare State and Family

In Europe, there has always been a 'toing and froing' between collective solidarity as realised by the welfare state and family-based relations and processes. A position on family is built into many welfare state policies – so much so that one can speak of welfare/family systems. Most developed welfare states operate with a set of preferences about family activities, relations and respective gender and generational roles. Such preferences are the stuff of 'family policy' but they pervade social policy more broadly as well and are to be found also in economic and employment policy. In some countries family is set up as an alternative to state intervention – this is a core meaning of the subsidiarity principle in the continental European countries. In Germany especially, the idea of subsidiarity is that the state as a high-level form of interest and organisation will only intervene after the family (or other so-called lower-level institutions) is allowed the space to act. So for example, German welfare state policies up until quite recently were organised so that they did not interfere with the classic functions of family (e.g. caring for and rearing children) and the traditional ways of organising family life that went along with that (father as breadwinner and mother based mainly in the home) (Ostner 1994; Bleses and Seeleib-Kaiser 2004).

Most countries, especially in Europe, have a wide portfolio of family-related policies. There are many possible goals of family policy just as there are many interpretations of the relationship between family policy and family life. Four classic motivations have driven state engagement with family policy: to influence or compensate for the effects of demographic change; to effect horizontal redistribution or equity between those with children and those without; to help alleviate poverty; to aim for gender equality (Wennemo 1994; Gauthier 1996). The significance and priority of each has varied over time and place, so much so that Europe has been said to have a number of models of family–state–market relations.[4] While space does not allow any real treatment of this, the overview provided in chapter 4 of welfare state variations covered some of this ground. It suggested a strongly pro-family (in general and also for the particular form of the nuclear married couple family) approach in Germany and neighbouring countries, a universalistic approach in Scandinavia which sees strong state support of individual income equality and the provision of care, limited family policy in the Mediterranean countries, and a 'targeted' approach in the UK and Ireland which focuses on needy families and on enabling self-sufficiency on the part of both individuals and families.

What are the contemporary emphases of policy?

While the cross-national differences in approach and the differentiated history of state policy on families must always be respected, one can identify a somewhat similar set of goals across countries in Europe at the present time. These are rather different to the policies pursued in the golden age (which in the case of family policies was somewhat later than in social security policy, occurring in the 1970s and early 1980s). During that time, the focus was on expanding female employment, providing out of home childcare and education, and gender equality. All of these were strongly endorsed by the EU and OECD. It now appears that in the last years especially many of the processes set in train in the earlier period are on hold, so much so that we may have entered a new phase of family policy. Today countries seem to have drawn back from gender equality as a goal, for example, and they have also tempered the movement to provide services that substitute for family care so that more women can be employed (Lewis 2006). While there is definitely a move away from a male breadwinner model, this is not being substituted for by a Scandinavian model whereby the state undertakes a form of socialisation of family tasks and functions. It seems that governments today consider that key aspects of welfare are best located in the family and that family itself should be promoted and protected. There is evidence of a new familism and a new instrumentalism. Children's well-being is very much to the fore and this is interpreted especially in terms of early education and human capital building (Scheiwe and Willekens 2009). In a kind of a mirror image of activation for adults, children, too, are expected to be active in the search after education. An uneducated childhood is a lazy childhood. Rather than moving care and welfare from the family, countries are endorsing a model of family life in which care is better shared among family members and with a range of providers outside the family. Hence, while women and men are encouraged to be workers, a gender hierarchy and division of labour remains and family as an institution and a locus of care is supported. Rather than an adult worker model, then, as predicted by Jane Lewis (2001), a dual earner, gender-specialised, family arrangement is being promoted. The long thread of conservatism in family policy seems to be continuing.

We turn now to the community as a source of welfare.

Civil Society, Support in the Community and Social Integration

The term 'civil society' typically refers to organisations that mediate between the state and individuals (Rose 2006). It includes such diverse groupings as political parties, trade unions, business associations, charitable bodies and religious, sports and cultural groups. While civil society organisations are conceived as independent of the state, their activities are often oriented to the public interest. They therefore resonate with democratic ideals and are generally seen to be welfare producing, not least in terms of their capacity to give voice, to secure respect for individuals and groups, and to mobilise 'resistance' to the formal political structure and interests. There is also another side to civil society organisations in that many are actively involved in service provision. Known as the third sector or the voluntary and community sector, it constitutes a significant domain of social and economic life. In the UK, for example:[5]

- In 2005 there were over 169,000 general charities and between 500,000 and 900,000 community organisations. The total income of charities was £31.0 billion in 2005/6.
- The voluntary sector employed 611,000 people in 2005.
- The number of people volunteering formally or informally at least once a month rose from 18.4 million in 2001 to 20.4 million in 2005. Formal volunteering in Great Britain is equivalent in monetary value to some £38 billion per year.
- Charitable giving has kept up with the growth in GDP in recent years, at around £9 billion in 2005–6.
- Research into charities estimates that turnover has increased from around £16 billion in 1997 to over £27 billion in 2004–5 and the workforce has increased by around a fifth.

- The total turnover of some 55,000 social enterprises is estimated at £27 billion, or 1.3 per cent of the total turnover of all businesses with employees. The annual contribution to GDP is estimated to be £8.4 billion.

A Eurobarometer Survey carried out in 2004 (and reported on in Rose 2006) indicates that involvement in voluntary activities is quite widespread in the EU. About 45 per cent of people report such involvement. The EU population falls into three groupings: 55 per cent do not belong to any organisation, 25 per cent belong to one particular organisation, and the remaining 20 per cent belong to two or more organisations. Sports clubs are the most popular type of organisational membership, with one in five respondents reporting that they are a member of a recreational organisation. Educational/arts, trade unions and religious organisations are the next most popular type of engagement, with some 10 per cent of respondents reporting belonging to these types of organisation. A significant minority of engagement is directly involved with politics, if one puts together engagement in political parties, groups concerned with international aid, the environment, consumer rights and causes such as women's rights.

Participation in voluntary organisations varies considerably across Europe, suggesting that there are national cultural norms of participation or non-participation. The Scandinavian countries have by far the highest level of participation – the average Swede is a member of three organisations, for example – and it is low in the Mediterranean and Eastern European countries (ibid.). The UK is slightly above the EU average with a national average of one membership. Among the factors that significantly influence participation in voluntary organisations are the extent to which the national government is perceived to be transparent and honest. Social class or educational background also affects participation (participation is higher among the better educated) (ibid.).

As we saw in chapter 2, a number of concepts have emerged in academic and policy circles to capture notions of social integration and the vibrancy of community. These approaches turn the attention on social and societal processes of integration and detachment; concerns with material subsistence are superseded by issues of social relations, normative systems and processes of participation.

Social exclusion is one way of approaching social integration and the community as a welfare-generating mechanism. Its conception of welfare emerged in part anyway from a critique of the state, especially in regard to poverty (Vobruba [2000], referred to in Phillips 2006: 115). Social exclusion is often claimed to be a superior concept to poverty – more multidimensional, more dynamic especially in that it has a focus on processes (rather than outcomes which are a characteristic focus of much poverty research), more social rather than economic or material, and more relational (as against distributional) (Phillips 2006: 117). However, it is probably not appropriate to compare them in this way as the two concepts originate from different sets of ideas. Poverty is an economic concept that has been widened to include a more social set of referents, whereas social exclusion is in origin and essence a concept about social relations and social membership (Silver 1994). However, Townsend's conceptualisation of poverty as an incapacity to participate in social and economic life according to contemporary norms and standards is a bridge between the two approaches (Rustin and Rix 1997: 15).

A defining element of social exclusion as a concept or approach is not just its interest in social problems and inequality but its sense of cumulation of different conditions of disadvantage – social, economic, political and even cultural factors are all involved. The concept therefore seeks to pick up on the extent to which different types of deprivation overlap and cumulate over time, especially in the context of a risk society. As Phillips (2006: 118) points out, there is a wide span of potential causes involved in social exclusion. But a systemic or societal critique is central: how key aspects of social systems fail to prevent or actually act to create and exacerbate social exclusion and marginalisation. The state is especially to the fore in these critiques. The democratic and legal system, the labour market, the welfare system and the family and community may all be implicated in social exclusion.

Empirically, social exclusion tends to lead to the study of the poor and marginalised. Studies typically consider the degree to which those who are economically deprived suffer from multiple forms of social deprivation. What is of especial relevance in the concept from the current perspective is the idea of inclusion in and attachment to the community. Böhnke (2008b) operationalises it as feeling recognised and valued and feelings of being included, participating and belonging. She finds that the majority of people feel included right across the EU, although people in the original fifteen member states are more likely than those in the new member states of Eastern, Mediterranean and Baltic Europe to have a sense of belonging. In Slovakia and Bulgaria, for example, some 40 per cent and 24 per cent of people respectively voice feelings of exclusion. Feeling of being respected and socially included is most widespread in the Nordic countries. Income level and having a job are closely associated with a sense of belonging in all countries. People who cannot rely on their family and a network of other support are less likely to feel they belong to society and the more reliable social support is the more people will see themselves as a respected member of society. The sense of belonging is generally more widespread in the affluent countries but then the gap in the sense of belonging between the economically privileged and the poor is smaller in the less affluent countries. It is said that in prosperous countries – where only relatively small minorities experience financial shortcomings – people are more likely to see personal failure rather than structural constraints as the explanation of their problem and this nourishes outsider feelings (ibid.: 317). But feeling left out of family is by far the strongest predictor of subjective social exclusion. Where such social networks do not exist, the services offered by the welfare state compensate for them.

Overview

While we have only been able to point in this chapter to how family and community can be welfare-generating, the discussion helps to portray these two multidimensional domains in a different manner to how they are normally represented. The family as a set of social relations and activities has many welfare-related sides to it – it generates welfare directly through care-related provision and the nurturing of personal relations and it affects welfare indirectly by virtue of the extent to which it engages in income management and redistribution. The family channels material resources (actual money exchanged on a regular basis or assets which are passed on through inheritance, for example). There is also a sense in which families generate material welfare by virtue of the activities they engage in. These include many types of unpaid work. Although these do not typically have a monetary value placed on them, they are of huge social and economic significance in their own right and when they are calculated in monetary terms. Immaterial resources are also generated by and passed on through families – we refer to feelings of security and support and also to somewhat 'harder' resources such as knowledge and social contacts. The underlying point overall is of the large role played by the family in generating and securing welfare.

Community activities and relations, too, are welfare-conferring in a number of senses. They are frequently engaged in service provision, for example (although this can be difficult to measure) and they are a site of participation and involvement. In the latter regard, they represent a source of social capital in the sense especially of improving social relations and quality of life.

7
Conclusion

This book has had three main objectives: to identify the meaning and relevance of welfare as a concept; to explore welfare as a focus of philosophical debate and political organisation; and, thirdly, to identify welfare as an aspect of people's individual endeavour and collective effort and shared institutions.

The essence of the first task was to examine welfare as an idea and object of theoretical thought. This was approached by tracing the historical origins and background to welfare and by juxtaposing it to other concepts and approaches. While it is used in very general ways in popular discourse, welfare's history in the social sciences is in particular sets of scholarship – in neo-classical economics, for example, it refers to the utilities or pleasure generated by market-based exchanges; in philosophy and political science it was developed as a contested ethical principle and focus of political organisation; and in the early life of the disciplines of Social Policy and social work welfare connoted social problems and the effectiveness of social institutions and other organised responses to need. Viewed in the round, the concept's original meanings are strong on material resources and the institutions and practices that govern access to resources and social aid. Welfare as a concept is also attuned to trajectories over time, how people fare as their lives unfold. The concept's clear focus on objective conditions is to be underlined in a period when social structural factors are under-emphasised in theory and research but count hugely in people's everyday lives. Furthermore, welfare is a concept that has purchase at both micro and macro levels and it works well in exploring the connections between these two levels (between the social organisation of the state and individual behaviour, for example). Above all, welfare taps into the nature of social divisions and opposing philosophical and political positions on how to address these and other phenomena.

However, welfare has been eclipsed by other concepts, especially in recent years by well-being and capabilities. These prioritise respectively individuals' subjective feelings and orientations and their capacities for action. These are now mainstream concepts, unlike one of the other alternative concepts we also considered – care – which, while widely used in feminist and some health and social service scholarship, remains on the sidelines of conventional thinking. The well-being and capabilities concepts appeal for their references to personhood and subjectivity on the one hand and agency and fulfilment (rather than resources) on the other. The reasons why welfare has come to be eclipsed merit analysis as they tell us something important about contemporary scholarship. Welfare appears too passive for the agency approaches and too oriented to subsistence and minimum for those that search after the richness and boundlessness of inner and outer lives in the highly developed world. Given the strong individualistic turn in scholarship, the concept of welfare seems too structure-bound and too oriented to the material level. The shift is only partly due to the innate appeal of the other concepts and the weaknesses of welfare when compared to them. Also significant has been the 'corruption' of welfare as a term – its dominant public register especially in the US has come to be the behaviours of those receiving public benefits which have been interpreted in a particularistic and negative fashion. There is also the fact that welfare is underdeveloped as a concept. Given the latter especially, we have in this book suggested that it is instructive to expand the concept on the basis of insights from the new scholarship.

Some of the newer concepts (e.g. well-being, social exclusion) have strengths where welfare is relatively silent – interpersonal relations and the connections between feeling and context are emphasised by the former, for example, while the latter aims for a more actor-centred approach in focusing on the extent to which people are engaged in a range of activities and relations (especially those which are considered core to a society). However, none of the new concepts alone is superior to welfare. This is true in two senses. First, they all have shortcomings and blind sides and, secondly, they are relatively weak on resource-holding and the meeting of collective need. In particular, welfare appears to be superior to concepts like subjective well-being and happiness. The latter are economically and politically shallow; they are too focused on the mindsets of individuals and conceive of social factors mainly as background conditions affecting individual functioning.

That said, there are genuine insights in some of the new scholarship and it does underline the risks of focusing too much on material situation and socio-economic position. Mindful of this, we have sought to develop the concept of welfare to take on a more relational and social cast, while retaining its original references to social structure and the distribution of material resources. We have suggested, then, that welfare be broadened to include a relational aspect. This means bringing into it an interest in caring as an activity and orientation and a concern with the extent to which people are participants in a range of domains. The case that we make for this broadened conception of welfare includes the following. First, using welfare as a frame allows one to capture core aspects of contemporary social and economic life. Secondly, it gives access to key oppositions in philosophical and political debate. Thirdly, a broadened conception of welfare leads to an improved reading of the architecture of social and economic life and how it is instrumental in shaping the contours and courses of people's everyday lives. In sum, the concept of welfare allows access to the systemic contexts for human well-being (broadly understood).

The second aim of the book was to consider welfare as a subject of philosophical debate and a goal of political action and organisation. In this regard, the chapters in the second part of the book showed how welfare fits with different philosophical positions and how, especially in the guise of the welfare state, it has been a focus of state/societal organisation in the highly developed world. Welfare is in fact a polarising notion – positions vary widely on the extent to which welfare should be understood as pertaining to individuals or to collective life in general and the extent to which welfare is a legitimate ground to open the public purse. The range of positions is book-ended on the one hand by perspectives of a liberal and neo-liberal orientation which hold that welfare is primarily an individual-level phenomenon and is best secured through market activities. At the other end are socialist perspectives which regard welfare as collective in nature and the legitimate object of public resource expenditure and state regulation and activity. The discussion focused especially on reform, mainly because it has been so prominent (predating the latest crisis by two decades or more). Welfare has been central to reform projects. It has been at the root of ideological change in terms of changing positions on collective welfare and also operational change in terms of how the organisation of welfare is actually changing across a range of countries.

The narrowness of existing visions of reform is striking. Neo-liberal discourses are dominant – they are the 'common sense' of our era and penetrate our lives in ways we do not even realise (Connell 2010: 22). While it is most familiar as a set of economic policies, the overall neo-liberal project is not just to stabilise the market but to extend capitalism and the market as widely as possible. When it comes to welfare and the welfare state, neo-liberalism seeks to integrate state and market operations more closely, mobilise the state on behalf of market agendas and reconfigure the state on market terms (Fording et al. 2009). For the real-life organisation of welfare, this spells a greater commodification of organised welfare – by subjecting it more and more to contract and provision by commercial interests – and greater privatisation of collective goods and collective objectives. What for thirty years or so after the Second World War was the other book-end – social democracy – has shifted much closer to neo-liberalism, hence the narrowing of the reform canvas. In the last decades especially, the parties of the centre-left (the so-called social democratic parties) have been almost as involved in the neo-liberal project as the parties of the right. Both readily engaged in projects of deregulation and other measures to create a financial regime wherein key players (like international corporations) operated virtually without public control. And while they sought to secure the minimum safety net and pursued 'pet projects' (such as New Labour's support of the family in the UK), they were instrumental in undermining the foundations of the post-war welfare state. Think of Clinton in the US, Blair and Brown in the UK and Schröder in Germany. Because social democracy was a party to the conditions that led to the current crisis, it lacks legitimacy and also ideas as an alternative project today. Indeed, the economic crisis is also a crisis of social democracy (Ryner 2010).

It is important, however, not to overstate the extent of the changes, especially in terms of the programmes and expenditures of the welfare state. While there is no doubt that a narrative of welfare state failure and culpability prevails, it is also the case that the welfare state is unlikely to be changed by ideology or politics alone, not in the short term anyway. The analysis carried out in the later chapters of this book shows that the welfare state is a form of societal organisation, rather than a political or ideological entity alone. Hence, it is widely institutionally embedded and is an important part of public expectations and the architecture of everyday life. If it did not exist we would have to invent it. Indeed, one could read some of the developments in the US around encouraging home ownership and improved lifestyles for the working poor and those on low to medium incomes by increased borrowing as suggesting the ubiquity of the need to put in place elements of a welfare architecture. While it was no accident that this was done by increasing the profitability and influence of the financial sector and miring the borrowers in debt, there was something in it also that was about substituting for a declining welfare state and people's need for security in that context.

This brings us to the third aim of the book: identifying welfare empirically. While handicapped by lacking data, the analyses carried out, especially those in chapters 5 and 6, were meant to enquire into some of the dimensions of welfare as an everyday concern at the present time. We wanted to show that welfare, especially in the broadened sense developed here, is a meaningful way of understanding aspects of real life and that it is illuminative of a range of existing practices, processes and institutions. In sum, welfare can be tracked to fundamental goals of a range of human agency around provisioning especially. Yet it is clear from the empirical analyses that welfare provision is not the preserve of any single domain or arena but rests on the interaction of (at least) four domains: family, state, market, community. There is a dynamic interplay at work, involving forms of social, political and economic organisation, ways of life and social relations.

While the analyses in this section of the book were intended mainly to demonstrate some of the range of application of welfare as a frame of analysis, they also revealed some key aspects of how far welfare is realised by the mass of the population. The limits of the market were especially revealed – unemployment, low pay, poor conditions for many workers as well as widespread insecurity in job tenure and prospects for advancement. The limits of the welfare state are also clear – poverty rates that extend widely and are growing, increasing income and other forms of inequality, and reduced chances of improving on one's socio-economic situation. These were not what the post-war welfare state in Europe was expanded to do. The virtuous cycle whereby economic growth was associated with progressive improvement in a range of welfare indicators has been broken. As Wilkinson and Pickett (2009: 5–6) put it: 'Economic growth, for so long the great engine of progress, has, in the rich countries, largely finished its work. ... The populations of rich countries have got to the end of a long historical journey.'

So we are now at an epochal moment (another one). To end, I would like to make two points.

First, a number of commentators have suggested that in the next generation of change in the welfare state it will be culture rather than economics or politics that will frame the changes (Rodger 2000; Heclo 2001). Rodger (2000), for example, suggests that politics and economics are no longer the pre-eminent forces shaping our thinking about social policy because it is culture, particularly values, lifestyles and emotional choices about caring and the welfare of others, that frames the way societies organise their welfare provision and the meaning they attach to it. I tend to disagree and suggest that as we go forward welfare will be as much about social life, politics and economics as it has ever been. As analysts, we have to keep connecting economic and political developments with society.

Secondly, as we ponder the future it is wise to remember that both welfare and the welfare state are the subject of many mythological reinterpretations (Deakin 1994: 51–4). The main myth, says Deakin (ibid.: 52), is the secular one of progress – at base a notion of an organic society that evolves and adapts and uses past experience to learn from and improve provision. A second myth is of that of settlement – that once measures are put in place they remain and are subject to no more seismic shifts. Both of these are conservative in origin, resting on a belief that the best future lies in the past. And they are both false. The analyses carried out in this book show that policies during the last fifty years have gone back and forth over the ground of welfare and that any consensus has been relatively short-lived. In particular, the consensus around the welfare state as a desired form of organisation, while it has not been undone, has become unfirm under the onslaught of neo-liberalism. All of this means that we would be ill advised to underestimate the extent to which questions about the detail and meaning of welfare are at the centre rather than the margins of political contest in the future.

Notes

Introduction

1 See http://www.eurofound.europa.eu.

Chapter 1   Founding Ideas and Approaches

1 See http://www.welfarism.com for information and a wide-ranging list of readings on welfarism, utilitarianism and related concepts.

2 For the sake of clarity, I capitalise the term 'Social Policy' when I am referring to the academic discipline.

3 The approach has proved enduring: the study of social problems has occupied a significant place in the development of sociology in both the UK and the US, especially continuing in the latter. American sociology, for example, has a sub-discipline devoted to the study of social problems. This has a strong deviance and social disorganisation focus (e.g., Rubington and Weinberg 1981). See also Manning (1985).

4 As in the poverty studies of Charles Booth in London in the 1880s and Seebohm Rowntree in York at the turn of the nineteenth to the twentieth century and in the 1930s, and in the US with studies in Chicago, Philadelphia and Pittsburgh (O'Connor 2001).

5 The historical evolution of Social Policy as a discipline in the UK is grounded in an attachment to the precepts and modes

of analysis of social administration. Its commitment to applied administrative science defined Social Policy as an empiricist discipline. It believed in the technocratic skills of social planners and administrators and considered rational social progress as possible and desirable. Social Policy also has an intellectual heritage in idealism and a commitment to collectivism (Bulmer et al. 1989). These are origins rather than current orientations, however. More recently, Social Policy has become so open to insights from and approaches of other disciplines that some deem it more appropriately characterised as a field than a discipline (Mishra 1989; Alcock 1996).

6   See Dean (2010) for a good overview.
7   There is an interesting literature on 'claims making' – for welfare-related claims making see Peattie and Rein (1983) and Drover and Kerans (1993) in particular.
8   See http://www.givingusa.org.

Chapter 2   Well-being and Other Challenges to Conventional Understandings of Welfare

1   See Layard (2005). There is now a World Database on happiness. See http://www.eur.nl/fsw/research/happiness.
2   There is a specific EU-wide survey oriented to this. The EU-funded European Quality of Life Survey was first carried out in 2003 and covered 28 European countries. A second round was carried out in 2007, covering 31 countries. An opinion survey, it is oriented especially to living conditions and quality of life, covering both subjective and objective aspects. Among the issues covered are employment, income, education, housing, family, health, work–life balance, life satisfaction and perceived quality of society. See http://www.eurofound.europa.eu/areas/qualityoflife/eqls/index.htm.
3   But Martha Nussbaum (2000) has used Sen's approach to devise a list of essential capabilities to live at a minimum decent level with dignity. Consciously building a basis for justice, core rights and universal human values, Nussbaum rejects subjective welfarism or utility and concludes that there are 11 human 'functional capacities': life (being able to live to the end of a normal human life), bodily health, bodily integrity, freedom of use of expression of senses, imagination and thought, emotions (to be able to feel without fear, anxiety, abuse or neglect), practical reason (able to form a conception of the good and to

engage in critical reflection), be able to interact and have friendships (affiliation), concern for other species, play, control over environment, being able to live one's life and nobody else's. See Gough (2003) for a critique of this and a comparison to his own (and Doyal's) theory of human need.

4   For a history of the Human Development Report see http://hdr.undp.org/en/humandev/reports/.

5   See also Offer (2006) and Halpern (2009).

6   Sociology has other relevant concepts also; in fact it is a rather crowded field. Social cohesion and social quality are two such concepts but these are not considered here mainly because their linkages to welfare are less direct. Phillips (2006) is an excellent source on these and other related concepts.

7   The EU Lisbon process, which started in 2000 and is due to end in 2010, has been a major forum for the development of the measurement of poverty and social exclusion. See Atkinson et al. (2002) and Marlier et al. (2007).

8   It dates from the 1960s and the War on Poverty programme of President Lyndon Johnson. It takes its departure point from research indicating that families spend about one-third of their income on food – the official poverty level was set by multiplying basic food costs by three. Since then, the figures have been updated annually for inflation but the process and the underlying reasoning have remained unchanged. Over time, as incomes have grown in real terms, the poverty threshold has fallen relative to average income – from 48 per cent of median family income in 1960 to 29 per cent in 2000 (Le Grand et al. 2008: 160). Note that in the EU, the customary cut-off poverty threshold is 60 per cent of median income.

9   A book on the subject by René Lenoir, published in 1974, was given the title *Les Exclus: Un Français sur dix* by the publisher.

10 See Chamberlayne (1997) for a very interesting discussion of social exclusion in the context of sociological approaches and heritages in a range of different European countries. As regards chameleon concepts, Beauvais and Jenson (2002) make a relevant point when they observe in relation to another concept with a range of meanings – social cohesion – that it seems to figure in policy discussions at the point when single-focus policies, such as anti-poverty, employment, community development, do not work as effectively as desired. In this and other ways, chameleon concepts serve the function of manipulating and modernising the discourse of social and economic policy.

11 See Phillips (2006: 119–21) and also Levitas (1998).

12 It should be noted, though, that social capital is another concept with origins in diverse sets of scholarship. The concept has three main interpretations: those of the sociologists James Coleman and Pierre Bourdieu and the political scientist Robert Putnam. Since the understandings of both Bourdieu and Putnam are discussed in the text, a word or two is appropriate here about the conception of James Coleman. Working in the sociology of education, Coleman (1988) developed social capital as a feature of social structure, its production a function of the structure of social relationships (their degree of closure) and their content (especially the extent to which they are multiplex). In Coleman's world, the features of social structure that facilitate actors' access to resources include reciprocity in relationships, channels of information, closed and multiplex social relations and appropriate social organisation. His claim is that people with such types of personal contact and relations are most likely to do better than those lacking them.

Chapter 3   Classic Political Philosophies of Welfare

1   There are, of course, other political philosophies. Feminism is an obvious case, not least because it has been strongly oriented to matters of welfare. Rather than considered in its own right, feminism is used as a basis to critique key assumptions of the mainstream philosophies.

2   Stated formally, Rawls's principles of justice are that 'each person should have the most extensive system of equal basic liberties compatible with similar liberties for all' and 'social and economic inequalities to be arranged so that they are (a) to the greatest advantage to the least advantaged consistent with a just savings principle, and (b) attached to choices and positions open to all under conditions of fair equality of opportunity' (Rawls 1971).

3   The term 'New Right' is widely used but it is in fact composed of two distinct strands of thought: economic and moral. The fact that it draws from two quite different sources – the former from neo-classical economics and the latter from a complex blend of social and ethical ideas – makes it a somewhat unreliable descriptor (Barry 1999b: 77–9).

4   Labels have to be treated with great care for, as Finlayson (1999) has observed, third way theory is not a political theory in the conventional sense but an attempt to think through the

implications of sociological theorising about change (especially in the work of Giddens (1994) and Beck (1992)). Jayasuriya terms this a particular kind of moral sociology in that description of modes of social conduct substitute for the ethical and political reasoning found in most political programmes (2006: 35). The term 'third way' has moved a good deal from its origins, which lie in the particularity of the Scandinavian welfare state model as a third way between the command economies of Eastern Europe and the market capitalism of the western nations in the post-Second World War period (Rodger 2000: 97–8).

5   This is a term applied to situations in which reducing the consequences of a risk event if it occurs increases the likelihood that the event will in fact occur (Walker 2005: 48–9). The case has been made, quite strongly in some quarters, that on being insured people tend to change their behaviour and reduce their efforts to avoid the risk (Le Grand et al. 2008: 170–1).

6   See Lister (2010: 49) for an outline of the meaning of these terms.

7   This to be tested in four areas initially. The trial areas announced on 19 July 2010 were Liverpool, Eden Valley Cumbria, Windsor and Maidenhead, and the London borough of Sutton. The initiatives involved included a local buy-out of a rural pub, efforts to recruit volunteers to keep museums open, support to speed up broadband supply, and giving residents more power over council spending ('David Cameron begins big sell of "big society"', *Guardian*, 19 July 2010).

Chapter 4   The State and Public Welfare

1   For welfare state theory, see Goodin (1998) and Pierson (2006) and for the latest theoretical and empirical thinking on welfare states see Castles et al. (2010).

2   See O'Connor et al. (1999).

Chapter 5   Securing Material Welfare through the Market and the State

1   The US data are calculated from the databases on the site of the Bureau of Labor Statistics at http://www.bls.gov/cps/cpsatabs.htm.

2   The European exceptions to the story of growing levels of female employment are some of the Eastern European countries where traditionally high rates of female employment have been stagnating or falling (mainly due to the difficulties associated with transition from a communist to a capitalist system).

3   These findings are based on men employed on a full-time basis and on data available from the following 11 countries: Canada, Finland, France, Germany, Japan, Korea, the Netherlands, New Zealand, Sweden, the UK and the US.

4   This statistic is the gender pay gap in unadjusted form which is based on the difference between the average gross hourly earnings of male and female paid employees shown as a share of men's earnings.

5   This includes temporary help agency workers, on-call workers, seasonal workers, and those on fixed contracts of one year or less.

6   Including much of it not considered directly in this chapter – the data and analyses presented in European Commission (2009b) give a good overview of trends.

7   There are other resonances in the term 'the working poor' as well. O'Connor (2000: 551) is of the view that it plays into an artificial and now largely outdated distinction between the employed ('deserving') and the welfare ('undeserving') poor.

8   The national minimum wage in 2009 was £5.80 for those over 22 years of age, £4.83 for those aged 18 to 21 and £3.57 for 16- and 17-year-olds.

9   The Gini coefficient relates to the distribution of income across the population. This (expressed as a percentage) takes a value of 0 in a situation of perfect equality wherein income is shared equally and 1 when income is totally unequal (when one person has all the income and all the rest have none, for example). The more it deviates from zero the more unequal the distribution. The most common values for the affluent countries tend to be between 0.2 and 0.4.

10   And even if it did we may not be able to identify it because panel data on income is not widely available for Europe. The European Community Household Panel Survey provided panel data for European Union countries from 1993 but was discontinued after 2001.

11   Unless otherwise stated, 'poverty' refers to the proportion of the population falling below an income threshold of 60 per cent of median income. This is in some cases referred to as low income or even as 'at risk of poverty' (under the auspices of the EU) but it is most widely recognised as an acceptable defini-

tion of poverty. It is a relative measure of poverty because the line moves with movement in the median income. This definition of poverty contrasts with absolute approaches, one example of which is the poverty line used by the US Census Bureau, which is calculated on the income required to purchase a fixed basket of food items, uprated in line with price changes (see chapter 2).

12   The income threshold per week was: £115 for a single adult with no dependent children, £199 for a couple with no dependent children, £195 for a single adult with two dependent children under 14 years and £279 for a couple with two dependent children under 14 years. See http://www.poverty.org.uk.

13   We consider here only income transfers, since the impact of services (such as health and education) is quite difficult to interpret at the level of the individual or household; but see OECD (2008).

14   See http://www.poverty.org.uk.

15   Poverty here is measured by a threshold of 50 per cent of the median income.

Chapter 6   The Personal and Social Relations of Welfare

1   GDP = private consumption + investment + government consumption + (exports – imports). It is based on a clear methodology that allows comparisons to be made over time and place. The internationally agreed framework and set of rules governing its calculation are set out, for the EU countries, in the European System of National Accounts, which are broadly consistent with the UN System of National Accounts. For a recent overview of the limitations of GDP see Stiglitz et al. (2009).

2   This work has typically proceeded along a number of lines but has especially converged around time-use surveys, the imputation of a monetary value to time spent on unpaid work and the creation of 'satellite accounts' to shadow the national accounts.

3   Becker's approach has been subject to major criticism from within and outside economics. Bergmann (1995) attacks Becker's assumption of specialisation for applying to the family a theoretical apparatus that has been developed to understand the functioning of markets. This means that behaviours that

take place within the family, such as marriage, childbearing and child-rearing, for example, are depicted as choices made by rational individuals whose motives are to maximise their own utility or pleasure.

4   See especially Bahle (2008).

5   See ESRC *Society Today* Third Sector Engagement Strategy at: http://www.esrc.ac.uk/ESRCInfoCentre/KnowledgeExch/ ESRCthirdsectorengagement.aspx. See also the Office of the Third Sector website in the Cabinet Office at: http://www .cabinetoffice.gov.uk/third_sector.aspx.

References

Adiseshiah, M. S. (1966) 'Welfare in economic thought: Some micro-economic propositions', in Morgan, J. S. (ed.) *Welfare and Wisdom*, Toronto: University of Toronto Press, pp. 97–116.

Albrow, M. (1993) 'The changing British role in European sociology', in Nedelmann, B. and Sztompka, P. (eds.) *Sociology in Europe In Search of Identity*, Berlin: Walter de Gruyter, pp. 81–97.

Alcock, P. (1996) *Social Policy in Britain: Themes and Issues*, Basingstoke: Macmillan.

Aliaga, C. (2006) 'How is the time of women and men distributed in Europe?', *Statistics in Focus Population and Social Conditions*, 4/2006, Eurostat.

Allin, P. (2007) 'Measuring societal wellbeing', *Economic and Labour Market Review*, 1, 10: 46–52.

Anderson, R., Mikulich, B., Vermeylen, G., Lyly-Yrjanainen, M. and Zigante, V. (2009) *Second European Quality of Life Survey Overview*, Luxembourg: European Foundation for the Improvement of Living and Working Conditions.

Anttonen, A. (2002) 'Universalism and social policy: A Nordic-feminist revaluation', *Nordic Journal of Women's Studies*, 10, 2: 71–80.

Atkinson, A., Cantillon, B., Marlier, E. and Nolan, B. (2002) *Social Indicators: The EU and Social Inclusion*, Oxford: Oxford University Press.

Bahle, T. (2008) 'Family policy patterns in the enlarged EU', in Alber, J., Fahey, T. and Saraceno, C. (eds.) *Handbook of Quality of Life in the Enlarged European Union*, London: Routledge, pp. 100–25.

Bahle, T. (2009) 'Public child care in Europe: Historical trajectories and new directions', in Scheiwe. K. and Willekens, H. (eds.) *Child Care and Preschool Development in Europe: Institutional Perspectives*, Basingstoke: Palgrave, pp. 23–42.

Baker, J., Lynch, K., Cantillon, S. and Walsh, J. (2004) *Equality: From Theory to Action*, Basingstoke: Palgrave.

Bane, M. J. and Ellwood, D. (1986) 'Slipping into and out of poverty: The dynamics of spells', *Journal of Human Resources*, 21, 1: 1–23.

Barry, N. (1990) *Welfare*, Buckingham: Open University Press.

Barry, N. (1999a) 'Neoclassicism, the new right and the British welfare state', in Page, R. M. and Silburn, R. L. (eds.) *British Social Welfare in the Twentieth Century*, Basingstoke: Macmillan, pp. 55–79.

Barry, N. (1999b) *Welfare*, 2nd edn, Milton Keynes: Open University Press.

Beauvais, C. and Jenson, J. (2002) *Social Cohesion: Updating the State of the Research*, CPRN Discussion Paper F22, Ottawa: Canadian Policy Research Networks.

Beck, U. (1992) Risk Society: *Towards a New Modernity*, London: Sage.

Beck, U. and Beck-Gernsheim, E. (1995) *The Normal Chaos of Love*, Cambridge: Polity.

Becker, G. S. (1981) *A Treatise on the Family*, Cambridge, MA: Harvard University Press.

Béland, D. and Waddan, A. (2007) 'Conservative ideas and social policy in the United States', *Social Policy & Administration*, 41, 7: 768–86.

Bergmann, B. (1995) 'Becker's theory of the family: Preposterous conclusions', *Feminist Economics*, 1, 1: 141–50.

Beveridge Report (1942) *Social Insurance and Allied Services*, Cmd 6404, London: HMSO.

Bianchi, S. M., Robinson, J. P. and Milkie, M. A. (2006) *Changing Rhythms of American Family Life*, New York: Russell Sage Foundation.

Blanden, J. and Gibbons, S. (2006) 'Cycles of disadvantage', *CentrePiece*, Summer: 27–8.

Blanden, J. and Machin, S. (2008) 'Up and down the generational income ladder in Britain: Past changes and future prospects', *National Institute Economic Review*, 205: 101–17.

Blanden, J., Gregg, P. and Machin, S. (2005) *Intergenerational Mobility in Europe and North America*, London: Centre for Economic Performance, London School of Economics.

Bleses, P. and Seeleib-Kaiser, M. (2004) *The Dual Transformation of the German Welfare State*, Basingstoke: Palgrave.

Blome, A., Keck, W. and Alber, J. (2009) *Family and the Welfare State in Europe Intergenerational Relations in Ageing Societies*, Cheltenham: Edward Elgar.

Böhnke, P. (2005) *First European Quality of Life Survey: Life Satisfaction, Happiness and Sense of Belonging*, Luxembourg: Office for Official Publications of the European Communities.

Böhnke, P. (2008a) 'Are the poor socially integrated? The link between poverty and social support in different welfare regimes', *Journal of European Social Policy*, 18, 2: 133–50.

Böhnke, P. (2008b) 'Feeling left out: Patterns of social integration and exclusion', in Alber, J., Fahey, T. and Saraceno, C. (eds.) *Handbook of Quality of Life in the Enlarged European Union*, London: Routledge, pp. 304–27.

Bourdieu, P. (1985) 'The forms of capital', in Richardson, J. G. (ed.) *Handbook of Theory and Research for the Sociology of Education*, New York: Greenwood Press, pp. 241–58.

Bradshaw, J. (1972) 'The concept of social need', *New Society*, 30 March.

Bradshaw, J. and Richardson, D. (2009) 'An index of child well-being in Europe', *Child Indicators Research*, 2, 3: 319–51.

Braedley, S. and Luxton, M. (2010) 'Competing philosophies: Neo-liberalism and challenges of everyday life', in Braedley, S. and Luxton, M. (eds.) *Neoliberalism and Everyday Life*, Quebec: McGill–Queen's University Press, pp. 3–21.

Breen, R. (ed.) (2004) *Social Mobility in Europe and the USA*, Oxford: Oxford University Press.

Brewer, M. and Gregg, P. (2003) 'Eradicating child poverty in Britain: Welfare reform and children since 1997', in Walker, R. and Wiseman, M. (eds.) *The Welfare We Want? The British Challenge for American Reform*, Bristol: Policy Press, pp. 81–114.

Brewer, M., Muriel, A., Phillips, D. and Sibieta, L. (2009) *Poverty and Inequality in the UK: 2009*, IFS Commentary 109, London: Institute for Fiscal Studies.

Briggs, A. (2000) 'The welfare state in historical perspective', in Pierson, C. and Castles, F. G. (eds.) *The Welfare State: A Reader*, Cambridge: Polity, pp. 18–31.

Bruni, L. and Porta, P. L. (eds.) (2005) *Economics and Happiness: Framing the Analysis*, Oxford: Oxford University Press.

Bulmer, M., Lewis, J., and Piachaud, D. (eds.) (1989) *The Goals of Social Policy*, London: Unwin Hyman.

Burchardt, T., Le Grand, J. and Piachaud, D. (2002) 'Degrees of exclusion: Developing a dynamic, multidimensional measure', in Hills, J., Le Grand, J. and Piachaud, D. (eds.) *Understanding Social Exclusion*, Oxford: Oxford University Press, pp. 30–43.

Burton, P., Phipps, S. and Woolley, F. (2007) 'Inequality within the household reconsidered', in Jenkins, S. P. and Micklewright, J. (eds.) *Inequality and Poverty Re-examined*, Oxford: Oxford University Press, pp. 103–25.

Byrne, D. (2005) *Social Exclusion*, 2nd edn, Milton Keynes: Open University Press.

Carers UK (2007) *Valuing Carers – Calculating the Value of Unpaid Care*, London: Carers UK.

Carmichael, F., Hulme, C., Sheppard, S. and Connell, G. (2008) 'Work–life imbalance: Informal care and paid employment in the UK', *Feminist Economics*, 14, 2: 3–35.

Castles, F. G. and Obinger, H. (2008) 'Worlds, families, regimes: Country clusters in European and OECD area public policy', *West European Politics*, 31, 1/2: 321–44.

Castles, F. G., Leibfried, S., Lewis, J., Obinger, H. and Pierson, C. (eds.) (2010) *The Oxford Handbook of the Welfare State*, Oxford: Oxford University Press.

Chamberlayne, P. (1997) 'Social exclusion: Sociological traditions and national contexts', in Chamberlayne, P. (ed.) *Social Strategies in Risk Societies*, SOSTRIS Working Paper 1, London: University of East London, pp. 1–11.

Clarke, J. (2004) *Changing Welfare, Changing States, New Directions in Social Policy*, London: Sage.

Clasen, J. (2005) *Reforming European Welfare States. Germany and the United Kingdom Compared*, Oxford: Oxford University Press.

Clayton, R. and Pontusson, J. (2000) 'Welfare state retrenchment revisited', in Pierson, C. and Castles, F. G. (eds.) *The Welfare State A Reader*, Cambridge: Polity, pp. 320–34.

Coleman, J. (1988) 'Social capital in the creation of human capital', *American Journal of Sociology*, 94: 95–120.

Commission on Social Justice (1994) *Social Justice*, London: Vintage.

Connell, R. (2010) 'Understanding neoliberalism', in Braedley, S. and Luxton, M. (eds.) *Neoliberalism and Everyday Life*, Quebec: McGill–Queen's University Press, pp. 22–36.

Culyer, A. J. (1990) 'Commodities, characteristics, of commodities, characteristics of people, utilities, and the quality of life', in Baldwin, S., Godfrey, C. and Propper, C. (eds.) *Quality of Life Perspectives and Policies*, London: Routledge, pp. 9–27.

Daly, M. (2000a) *The Gender Division of Welfare*, Cambridge: Cambridge University Press.

Daly, M. (2000b) 'A fine balance? Women's labour market participation patterns in international comparison', in Scharpf, F. and

Schmidt, V. (eds.) *From Vulnerability to Competitiveness: Welfare and Work in the Open Economy*, vol. 2, Oxford: Oxford University Press, pp. 467–510.

Daly, M. (2006) 'EU social policy after Lisbon', *Journal of Common Market Studies*, 44, 3: 461–81.

Daly, M. and Leonard, M. (2002) *Against All Odds: Family Life on Low Income in Ireland*, Dublin: Institute of Public Administration.

Daly, M. and Lewis, J. (2000) 'The concept of social care and the analysis of contemporary welfare states', *British Journal of Sociology*, 51, 2: 281–98.

Daly, M. and Rake, K. (2003) *Gender and the Welfare State: Care, Work and Welfare in Europe and the USA*, Cambridge: Polity.

Daly, M. and Silver, H. (2008) 'Social exclusion and social capital: A comparison and critique', *Theory and Society*, 37, 6: 537–66.

Deacon, A. (2002) *Perspectives on Welfare*, Milton Keynes: Open University Press.

Deacon, A. (2003) 'The British perspective on reform: Transfers from, and a lesson for, the US', in Walker, R. and Wiseman, M. (eds.) *The Welfare We Want? The British Challenge for American Reform*, Bristol: Policy Press, pp. 65–80.

Deakin, N. (1994) *The Politics of Welfare Continuities and Change*, Hemel Hempstead: Harvester Wheatsheaf.

Deakin, N., Jones-Finer, C. and Matthews, B. (2004) 'General introduction', in Deakin, N., Jones-Finer, C. and Matthews, B. (eds.) *Welfare and the State Critical Concepts in Political Science*, 51, *Welfare States and Societies in the Making*, London: Routledge, pp. 1–7.

Dean, H. (2002) *Welfare Rights and Social Policy*, Harlow: Pearson Education.

Dean, H. (2006) *Social Policy*, Cambridge: Polity.

Dean, H. (2008) 'Imagining a eudaimonic ethic of social security', in Bradshaw, J. (ed.) *Social Security, Happiness and Well-being*, Antwerp: Intersentia, pp. 57–76.

Dean, H. (2010) *Understanding Human Need: Social Issues, Policy and Practice*, Bristol: Policy Press.

De Leonardis, O. (1993) 'New patterns of collective action in a "post-welfare" society: The Italian case', in Drover, G. and Kerans, P. (eds.) *New Approaches to Welfare Theory*, Aldershot: Edward Elgar, pp. 177–89.

Delhey, J. (2004) *Life Satisfaction in an Enlarged Europe*, Luxembourg: Office for Official Publication of the European Communities.

De Swaan, A. (1988) *In Care of the State Health Care, Education and Welfare in Europe and the USA in the Modern Era*, Oxford: Oxford University Press.

Devine, F., Savage, M., Scott, J. and Crompton, R. (eds.) (2005) *Rethinking Class: Identities, Cultures and Lifestyles*, Basingstoke: Palgrave.

Diener, E. (1984) 'Subjective well-being', *Psychological Bulletin*, 95: 542–75.

Diener, E. and Lucas, R. E. (1999) 'Personality and subjective well-being', in Kahneman, D., Diener, E. and Schwartz, N. (eds.) *Well-being: The Foundations of Hedonic Psychology*, New York: Russell Sage Foundation, pp. 213–29.

Donath, S. (2000) 'The other economy: A suggestion for a distinctly feminist economics', *Feminist Economics*, 6, 1: 115–23.

Doyal, L. and Gough, I. (1991) *A Theory of Human Need*, New York: Guildford Press.

Drake, R. F. (2001) *The Principles of Social Policy*, Basingstoke: Palgrave.

Drover, G. and Kerans, P. (1993) 'New approaches to welfare theory: Foundations', in Drover, G. and Kerans, P. (eds.) *New Approaches to Welfare Theory*, Aldershot: Edward Elgar, pp. 3–30.

Duménil, G. and Lévy, D. (2004) 'Neoliberal income trends: Wealth, class and ownership in the USA', *New Left Review*, 30: 105–33.

Duménil, G. and Lévy, D. (2009) *The Crisis of Neoliberalism and U.S. Hegemony*, available at: http://www.jourdan.ens.fr/levy/biblioa.htm (accessed 11 August 2010).

Dwyer, P. (2000) *Welfare Rights and Responsibilities Contesting Social Citizenship*, Bristol: Policy Press.

Easterlin, R. A. (1974) 'Does economic growth improve the human lot?', in David, P. A. and Reder, M. W. (eds.) *Nations and Households in Economic Growth: Essays in Honor of Moses Abramovitz*, New York: Academic Press.

Erikson, R. and Goldthorpe, J. (1992) *The Constant Flux: A Study of Class Mobility in Industrial Societies*, Oxford: Clarendon Press.

Esping-Andersen, G. (1990) *The Three Worlds of Welfare Capitalism*, Cambridge: Polity.

Etzioni, A. (1995) *The Spirit of Community: Rights, Responsibilities and the Communitarian Agenda*, London: Fontana.

Etzioni, A. (1998) 'Introduction', in Etzioni, A. (ed.) *The Essential Communitarian Reader*, Oxford: Rowman and Littlefield, pp. ix–xxiv.

European Commission (2009a) *Joint Report on Social Protection and Social Inclusion 2009*, Commission Staff Working Document, SEC (2009) 141, final, Brussels: European Commission.

European Commission (2009b) *Employment in Europe 2009*, Luxembourg: Office for Official Publications of the European Communities.

Eurostat (2010a) 'Labour Force Survey', *Newsrelease*, 117/2010, 4 August 2010 (available at: http://epp.eurostat.ec.europa.eu/cache/ITY_PUBLIC/3-04082010-BP/EN/3-04082010-BP-EN.PDF), accessed: 13 August 2010.

Eurostat (2010b) *Combating Poverty and Social Exclusion: A Statistical Portrait of the European Union 2010*, Luxembourg: Publications Office of the European Union.

Fahey, T., Nolan, B. and Whelan, C. (2003) *Monitoring Quality of Life in Europe*, Dublin: European Foundation for the Improvement of Living and Working Conditions.

Feder Kittay, E. (1999) *Love's Labour: Essays on Women, Equality, and Dependency*, New York: Routledge.

Felce, D. and Perry, J. (1995) 'Quality of life: Its definition and measurement', *Research in Developmental Disabilities*, 16, 1: 51–74.

Ferrera, M. (1996) 'The "southern model" of welfare in social Europe', *Journal of European Social Policy*, 6, 1: 17–37.

Finch, J. and Groves, D. (eds.) (1983) *A Labour of Love: Women, Work and Caring*, London: Routledge.

Finlayson, A. (1999) 'Third way theory', *Political Quarterly*, 3: 271–9.

Fitzpatrick, T. (2001) *Welfare Theory*, Basingstoke: Palgrave.

Fitzpatrick, T. (2005) *New Theories of Welfare*, Basingstoke: Palgrave.

Fives, A. (2008) *Political and Philosophical Debates in Welfare*, Basingstoke: Palgrave.

Folbre, N. (1986) 'Hearts and spades: Paradigms of household economics', *World Development*, 14, 2: 245–55.

Fording, R. C., Schram, S. F. and Soss, J. (2009) 'Governing the Poor: The Rise of the Neoliberal Paternalist State', APSA 2009 Toronto Meeting Paper (available at: http://ssrn.com/abstract=1449997, accessed: 18 July 2010).

Foucault, M. (1985) *Madness and Civilization*, New York: Pantheon Books.

Foucault, M. (1991) 'Governmentality', in Burchell, G., Gordon, C. and Miller, P. (eds.) *The Foucault Effect: Studies in Governmentality*, Hemel Hempstead: Harvester Wheatsheaf, pp. 87–104.

Frankel, C. (1966) 'The moral framework of the idea of welfare', in Morgan, J. S. (ed.) *Welfare and Wisdom*, Toronto: University of Toronto Press, pp. 147–64.

Frankena, W. K. (1962) 'The concept of social justice', in Brandt, R. B. (ed.) *Social Justice*, Englewood Cliffs, NJ: Prentice Hall, pp. 1–29.

Fraser, D. (2009) *The Evolution of the British Welfare State*, 4th edn, Basingstoke: Palgrave.

Fraser, N. (1989) *Unruly Practices*, Cambridge: Polity.

Fraser, N. (2001) 'Recognition without ethics?', *Theory, Culture and Society*, 18, 2/3: 21–42.

Fraser, N. (2003) 'Social justice in the age of identity politics: Redistribution, recognition and participation', in Fraser, N. and Honneth, A. *Redistribution or Recognition? A Political-Philosophical Exchange*, London: Verso, pp. 7–109.

Fraser, N. and Gordon, L. (1994a) 'A genealogy of *Dependency*: Tracing a keyword of the U.S. welfare state', *Signs*, 19, 2: 309–36.

Fraser, N. and Gordon, L. (1994b) 'Civil citizenship against social citizenship? On the ideology of contract versus charity', in Van Steenbergen, B. (ed.) *The Condition of Citizenship*, London: Sage, pp. 90–107.

Fraser, N. and Honneth, A. (2003) *Redistribution or Recognition? A Political Philosophical Exchange*, London: Verso.

Friedman, M. (1962) *Capitalism and Freedom*, Chicago: University of Chicago Press.

Furstenberg, F. F. and Kaplan, S. B. (2004) 'Social capital and the family', in Scott, J., Treas, J. and Richards, M. (eds.) *The Blackwell Companion to the Sociology of Families*, Oxford: Blackwell, pp. 218–32.

Gasper, D. (2007) 'Human well-being: Concepts and conceptualisations', in McGillivray, M. (ed.) *Human Well-being Concept and Measurement*, Basingstoke: Palgrave, pp. 23–64.

Gauthier, A. H. (1996) *The State and the Family: A Comparative Analysis of Family Policies in Industrialized Countries*, Oxford: Clarendon Press.

George, V. and Wilding, P. (1993) *Welfare and Ideology*, Hemel Hempstead: Harvester Wheatsheaf.

Giddens, A. (1994) *Beyond Left and Right: The Future of Radical Politics*, Cambridge: Polity.

Giddens, A. (1998) *The Third Way: The Renewal of Social Democracy*, Cambridge: Polity.

Gilligan, C. (1982) *In a Different Voice*, Cambridge, MA: Harvard University Press.

Glennerster, H. (1989) 'Swimming against the tide: The prospects for social policy?', in Bulmer, M., Lewis, J. and Piachaud, D. (eds.) *The Goals of Social Policy*, London: Unwin Hyman, pp. 108–28.

Glennerster, H. (2004) 'The context for Rowntree's contribution', in Glennerster, H., Hills, J., Piachaud, D. and Webb. J. (eds.) *One Hundred Years of Poverty and Policy*, York: Joseph Rowntree Foundation, pp. 15–28.

Goldthorpe, J. and Jackson, M. (2007) 'Intergenerational class mobility in contemporary Britain: Political concerns and empirical findings', *British Journal of Sociology*, 58: 526–46.

Goodin, R. E. (1998) *Reasons for Welfare: The Political Theory of the Welfare State*, Princeton: Princeton University Press.

Goodin, R. E., Le Grand, J. with Dryzek, J. (1987) *Not Only the Poor: The Middle Classes and the Welfare State*, London: Allen and Unwin.

Goodman, P. S. (2010) 'Millions of unemployed face years without jobs', *New York Times*, 21 Feb.

Gordon, D., Levitas, R. and Pantazis, C. (eds.) (2004) *Poverty and Social Exclusion in Britain*, Bristol: Policy Press.

Gough, I. (1979) *The Political Economy of the Welfare State*, London: Macmillan.

Gough, I. (2003) *Lists and Thresholds: Comparing the Doyal-Gough Theory of Human Need with Nussbaum's Capabilities Approach*, WeD Working Paper 1, Bath: ESRC Group on Wellbeing in Developing Countries.

Gough, I. (2008) 'European welfare states: Explanations and lessons for developing countries', in Dani, A. A. and de Haan, A. (eds.) *Inclusive States: Social Policy and Structural Inequalities*, Washington, DC: International Bank for Reconstruction and Development/World Bank, pp. 39–72.

Gough, I. and Therborn, G. (2010) 'The global futures of welfare states', in Castles, F. G., Leibfried, S., Lewis, J., Obinger, H. and Pierson, C. (eds.) *The Oxford Handbook of the Welfare State*, Oxford: Oxford University Press, pp. 762–80.

Graham, H. (1983) 'Caring: A labour of love', in Finch, J. and Groves, D. (eds.) *A Labour of Love*, London: Routledge & Kegan Paul, pp. 13–30.

Gray, J. (1983) 'Classical liberalism, positional goods and the politicization of poverty', in Ellis, A. and Kumar, K. (eds.) *Dilemmas of Liberal Democracies*, London: Tavistock, pp. 174–84.

Green, T. H. (1906) *Prolegomena to Ethics*, 5th edn, Oxford: Clarendon Press.

Griggs, J. and Walker, R. (2008) *The Costs of Child Poverty for Individuals and Societies: A Literature Review*, York: Joseph Rowntree Foundation.

Hacker, J. S. (2008) *The Great Risk Shift: The New Economic Insecurity and the Decline of the American Dream*, New York: Oxford University Press.

Halpern, D. (2009) *The Hidden Wealth of Nations*, Cambridge: Polity.

Handler, J. F. and Hasenfeld, Y. (1991) *The Moral Construction of Poverty Welfare Reform in America*, Newbury Park, CA: Sage.

Handler, J. F. and Hasenfeld, Y. (2007) *Blame Welfare, Ignore Poverty and Inequality*, New York: Cambridge University Press.

Harris, J. (1992) 'Political thought and the welfare state 1870–1940: An intellectual framework for British social policy', *Past and Present*, 135: 116–41.

Harris, J. (2009) ' "Social evils and social problems" in Britain since 1904', in Utting, D. (ed.) *Contemporary Social Evils*, Bristol: Policy Press, pp. 5–24.

Haworth, J. and Hart, G. (2007) 'Introduction', in Haworth, J. and Hart, G. (eds.) *Well-being: Individual, Community and Social Perspectives*, Basingstoke: Palgrave, pp. 1–22.

Hay, J. R. (1975) *The Origins of the Liberal Welfare Reforms, 1906–1914*, London: Macmillan.

Hayek, F. A. (1960) *The Constitution of Liberty*, Chicago: University of Chicago Press.

Hayek, F. A. (1976) *Law, Legislation and Liberty: The Mirage of Social Justice*, vol. 2, Chicago: University of Chicago Press.

Heclo, H. (1986) 'General welfare and two American political traditions', *Political Science Quarterly*, 101, 2: 179–96.

Heclo, H. (2001) 'The future of social policy making', in Ben-Arieh, A. and Gal, J. (eds.) *Into the Promised Land Issues Facing the Welfare State*, Westport, CT: Praeger, pp. 259–79.

Held, V. (2005) *The Ethics of Care: Personal, Political, and Global*, New York: Oxford University Press.

Hewitt, M. (1998) 'Social policy and human need', in Ellison, N. and Pierson, C. (eds.) *Developments in British Social Policy*, Basingstoke: Macmillan, pp. 61–77.

Hills, P. and Argyle, M. (2002) 'The Oxford Happiness Questionnaire: A compact scale for the measurement of psychological well-being', *Personality and Individual Difference*, 33, 7: 1073–82.

Hills, J., Smithies, R. and McKnight, A. (2006) *Tracking Income: How Working Families' Incomes Vary through the Year*, CASEreport 32, London: London School of Economics.

Hills, J., Sefton, T. and Stewart, K. (2009) 'Conclusions: Climbing every mountain or retreating from the foothills?', in Hills, J., Sefton, T. and Stewart, K. (eds.) *Towards a More Equal Society: Poverty, Inequality and Policy since 1997*, Bristol: Policy Press, pp. 341–59.

Hills, J., et al. (2010) *An Anatomy of Economic Inequality in the UK: Report of the National Equality Panel*, London: Government Equalities Office.

Hobhouse, L. T. (1922) *The Elements of Social Justice*, London: Allen and Unwin.

Honneth, A. (2004) 'Recognition and justice', *Acta Sociologica*, 47, 4: 351–64.

Hook, J. L. (2006) 'Care in context: Men's unpaid work in 20 countries, 1965–2003', *American Sociological Review*, 71, 4: 639–60.

Hurst, E., Guryan, J. and Kearney, M. (2008) *Parental Education and Parental Time Use*, Cambridge, MA: National Bureau of Economic Research Working Paper 13993.

Hutton, W. (1995) 'The 30/30/40 labour market', *The Jobs Letter*, 30, 15 December.

ILO (2009a) *Global Wage Report 2008/09*, Geneva: ILO.

ILO (2009b) *World of Work Report 2009: The Global Jobs Crisis and Beyond*, Geneva: ILO.

Irwin, S. and Williams, F. (2002) 'Understanding social values and social change: The case of care, family and intimacy', paper presented to ESPRN Conference on Social Values, Social Policies, University of Tilburg, 29–31 August.

Isin, E. F. and Wood, P. K. (1999) *Citizenship and Identity*, London: Sage.

Jayasuriya, K. (2006) *Statecraft, Welfare and the Politics of Inclusion*, Basingstoke: Palgrave.

Jencks, C. (2002) 'Does inequality matter?' *Daedalus*, Winter: 49–65.

Jones-Finer, C. (2004) 'Introduction to Volume 1', in Deakin, N., Jones-Finer, C., and Matthews, B. (eds.) *Welfare and the State: Critical Concepts in Political Science, 51, Welfare States and Societies in the Making*, London: Routledge, pp. 9–14.

Jordan, B. (2008a) *Welfare and Well-being: Social Value in Public Policy*, Bristol: Policy Press.

Jordan, B. (2008b) 'Income, involvement and well-being: The benefits and costs of interdependence', in Bradshaw, J. (ed.) *Social Security, Happiness and Well-being*, Antwerp: Intersentia, pp. 41–56.

Kawachi, I. and Berkman, L. (2000) 'Social cohesion, social capital and health', in Berkman, L. and Kawachi, I. (eds.) *Social Epidemiology*, New York: Oxford University Press, pp. 174–90.

Kearns, K. (1997) 'Social democratic perspectives on the welfare state', in Lavalette, M. and Pratt, A. (eds.) *Social Policy: A Conceptual and Theoretical Introduction*, London: Sage, pp. 11–30.

Kempson, E., Bryson, A. and Rowlingson, K. (1994) *Hard Times?* London: Policy Studies Institute.

Kidd, A. (2004) 'The state and pauperism', in Deakin, N., Jones-Finer, C. and Matthews, B. (eds.) *Welfare and the State Critical Concepts in Political Science*, London: Routledge, pp. 168–226.

Kohli, M. (1999) 'Private and public transfers between generations: Linking the family and the state', *European Societies*, 1, 1: 81–104.

Korpi, W. (1983) *The Democratic Class Struggle*, London: Routledge & Kegan Paul.

Lareau, A. (2003) *Unequal Childhoods Class, Race, and Family Life*, Berkeley: University of California Press.

Lavalette, M. (1997) 'Marx and the Marxist critique of welfare', in Lavalette, M. and Pratt, A. (eds.) *Social Policy A Conceptual and Theoretical Introduction*, London: Sage, pp. 50–79.

Layard, R. (2005) *Happiness Lessons from a New Science*, New York: Penguin.

Le Grand, J., Propper, C. and Smith, S. (2008) *The Economics of Social Problems*, 4th edn, Basingstoke: Palgrave.

Leira, A. (1992) *Welfare States and Working Mothers: The Scandinavian Experience*, Cambridge: Cambridge University Press.

Leisering, L. and Leibfried, S. (1999) *Time and Poverty in Western Welfare States: United Germany in Perspective*, Cambridge: Cambridge University Press.

Leisering, L. and Walker, R. (1998) 'Making the future: From dynamics to policy agendas', in Leisering, L. and Walker, R. (eds.) *The Dynamics of Modern Society Poverty, Policy and Welfare*, Bristol: Policy Press, pp. 263–85.

Lenoir, R. (1974) *Les Exclus: Un Français sur dix*, Paris: Seuil.

Leonard, P. (1997) *Postmodern Welfare Reconstructing an Imaginary Project*, London: Sage.

Levitas, R. (1998) *The Inclusive Society? Social Exclusion and New Labour*, Basingstoke: Palgrave.

Levitas, R., Pantazis, C., Fahmy, E., Gordon, D., Lloyd, E. and Patsios, D. (2007) *The Multi-dimensional Analysis of Social Exclusion*, Bristol: Department of Sociology and School for Social Policy, Townsend Centre for the International Study of Poverty and Bristol Institute for Public Affairs, University of Bristol.

Lewis, G. (2000) *'Race', Gender, Social Welfare*, Cambridge: Polity.

Lewis, J. (1992) 'Gender and the development of welfare regimes', *Journal of European Social Policy*, 2, 3: 159–73.

Lewis, J. (2001) 'The decline of the male breadwinner model: Implications for work and care', *Social Politics*, 8, 2: 152–69.

Lewis, J. (2006) 'Work/family reconciliation, equal opportunities and social policies: The interpretation of policy trajectories at the EU level and the meaning of gender equality', *Journal of European Public Policy*, 13, 3: 420–37.

Lister, R. (2003) *Citizenship: Feminist Perspectives*, 2nd edn, Basingstoke: Palgrave.

Lister, R. (2004) *Poverty*, Cambridge: Polity.

Lister, R. (2010) *Understanding Theories and Concepts in Social Policy*, Bristol: Policy Press.

Lowe, R. (1999) 'Introduction: The road from 1945', in Fawcett, H. and Lowe, R. (eds.) *Welfare Policy in Britain: The Road from 1945*, Basingstoke: Macmillan, pp. 1–17.

Lupton, R., Heath, N. and Salter, E. (2009) 'Education: New labour's top priority', in Hills, J., Sefton, T. and Stewart, K. (eds.) *Towards a More Equal Society? Poverty, Inequality and Policy since 1997*, Bristol: Policy Press, pp. 71–90.

Lynch, K., Baker, J. and Lyons, M. (2009) *Affective Equality Love, Care and Injustice*, Basingstoke: Palgrave.

McGillivray, M. (2007) 'Human well-being: Issues, concepts and measures', in McGillivray, M. (ed.) *Human Well-being Concept and Measurement*, Basingstoke: Palgrave, pp. 1–22.

Mack, J. and Lansley, S. (1985) *Poor Britain*, London: Unwin Hyman.

Mahon, R. (2006) 'The OECD and the work/family reconciliation agenda: Competing frames', in Lewis, J. (ed.) *Children, Changing Families and Welfare States*, Cheltenham: Edward Elgar, pp. 173–97.

Mann, K. (2009) 'Remembering and rethinking the social divisions of welfare 50 years on', *Journal of Social Policy*, 38, 1: 1–18.

Manning, N. (1985) 'Constructing social problems', in Manning, N. (ed.) *Social Problems and Welfare Ideology*, Aldershot: Gower, pp. 1–28.

Marlier, E., Atkinson, A. B., Cantillon, B. and Nolan, B. (2007) *The EU and Social Inclusion: Facing the Challenges*, Bristol: Policy Press.

Marshall, T. H. (1950) *Citizenship and Social Class, and Other Essays*, Cambridge: Cambridge University Press.

Martin, C. (2004) 'The rediscovery of family solidarity', in Knijn, T. and Komter, A. (eds.) *Solidarity between the Sexes and the*

Generations: Transformations in Europe, Cheltenham: Edward Elgar, pp. 3–17.

Maslow, A. (1970) *The Farther Reaches of the Human Mind*, New York: Viking Press.

Mayer, K. U. (1986) 'Structural constraints on the life course', *Human Development*, 29: 163–71.

Mead, L. M. (1986) *Beyond Entitlement: The Social Obligations of Citizenship*, New York: Free Press.

Megone, C. (1990) 'The quality of life starting from Aristotle', in Baldwin, S., Godfrey, C. and Propper, C. (eds.) *Quality of Life Perspectives and Policies*, London: Routledge, pp. 28–41.

Mishra, R. (1989) 'The academic tradition in social policy: The Titmuss years', in Bulmer, M., Lewis, J. and Piachaud, D. (eds.) *The Goals of Social Policy*, London: Unwin Hyman, pp. 64–83.

Mishra, R. (1990) *The Welfare State in Capitalist Society*, Hemel Hempstead: Harvester Wheatsheaf.

Munzi, T. and Smeeding, T. (2008) 'Conditions of social vulnerability, work and low income: Evidence for Europe in comparative perspective', in Costabile, L. (ed.) *Institutions for Social Well-being: Alternatives for Europe*, Basingstoke: Palgrave, pp. 33–73.

Murray, C. (1984) *Losing Ground American Social Policy 1950–1980*, New York: Basic Books.

Narayan, D. (2000) *Voices of the Poor: Can Anyone Hear Us?* Oxford: Oxford University Press for the World Bank.

Nisbet, R. (1986) *Conservatism*, Milton Keynes: Open University Press.

Nussbaum, M. (2000) *Women and Human Development: The Capabilities Approach*, Cambridge: Cambridge University Press.

O'Brien, M. and Penna, S. (1998) *Theorising Welfare: Enlightenment and Modern Society*, London: Sage.

O'Connor, A. (2001) *Poverty Knowledge: Social Science, Social Policy, and the Poor in Twentieth Century U.S. History*, Princeton: Princeton University Press.

O'Connor, J. S., Orloff, A. S. and Shaver, S. (1999) *States, Markets, Families, Gender, Liberalism and Social Policy*, Cambridge: Cambridge University Press.

OECD (2008) *Growing Unequal? Income Distribution and Poverty in OECD Countries*, Paris: OECD.

OECD (2009) 'In-work poverty: What can governments do?' *Policy Brief*, Paris: OECD.

Offe, C. (1984) *Contradictions of the Welfare State*, Cambridge, MA: MIT Press.

Offer, A. (2006) *The Challenge of Affluence Self-control and Well-being in the United States and Britain since 1950*, Oxford: Oxford University Press.

Office for National Statistics (2009a) *Wealth in Great Britain: Main Results from the Wealth and Assets Survey 2006/8*, Newport: ONS.

Office for National Statistics (2009b) 'The effects of taxes and benefits on household income, 2007/08', *Statistical Bulletin*, 29 July, Newport: ONS.

Orton, M. and Rowlingson, K. (2007) 'A problem of riches: Towards a new social policy research agenda on the distribution of economic resources', *Journal of Social Policy*, 36, 1: 59–77.

Ostner, I. (1994) 'Back to the fifties: Gender and welfare in unified Germany', *Social Politics*, 1, 1: 32–59.

Outhwaite, W. (2008) *European Society*, Cambridge: Polity.

Pahl, J. (1989) *Money and Marriage*, New York: St Martin's Press.

Parsons, T. and Bales, R. F. (1955) *Family Socialization and Interaction Process*, Glencoe, IL: Free Press.

Pateman, C. (1988) *The Sexual Contract*, Cambridge: Polity.

Paugam, S. (1991) *La Disqualification sociale. Essai sur la nouvelle pauvreté*, Paris: Presses Universitaires Françaises.

Peattie, L. and Rein, M. (1983) *Women's Claims: A Study in Political Economy*, Oxford: Oxford University Press.

Phillips, D. (2006) *Quality of Life Concept, Policy and Practice*, London: Routledge.

Pierson, C. (2006) *Beyond the Welfare State? The New Political Economy of Welfare*, 2nd edn, Cambridge: Polity.

Pinker, R. (1998) 'The conservative tradition of social welfare', in Alcock, P., Erskine, A. and May, M. (eds.) *The Students' Companion to Social Policy*, Oxford: Blackwell, pp. 64–70.

Piven, F. and Cloward, R. (1971) *Regulating the Poor: The Functions of Public Welfare*, New York: Pantheon.

Plant, R., Lesser, H. and Taylor-Gooby, P. (1980) *Political Philosophy and Social Welfare Essays on the Normative Basis of Welfare Provision*, London: Routledge & Kegan Paul.

Pratt, A. (1997) 'Neo-liberalism and social policy', in Lavalette, M. and Pratt, A. (eds.) *Social Policy A Conceptual and Theoretical Introduction*, London: Sage, pp. 31–49.

Prideaux, S. (2005) *Not So New Labour: A Sociological Critique of New Labour's Policy and Practice*, Bristol: Policy Press.

Pusić, E. (1966) 'The political community and the future of welfare', in Morgan, J. S. (ed.) *Welfare and Wisdom*, Toronto: University of Toronto Press, pp. 61–94.

Putnam, R. (1993) *Making Democracy Work: Civic Traditions in Modern Italy*, Princeton: Princeton University Press.

Putnam, R. (2000) *Bowling Alone: The Collapse and Revival of American Community*, New York: Simon and Schuster.

Rawls, J. (1971) *A Theory of Justice*, Cambridge, MA: Harvard University Press.

Ringen, S. (2007) *What Democracy is For: On Freedom and Moral Government*, Princeton: Princeton University Press.

Ritter, G. A. (1986) *Social Welfare in Germany and Britain*, Leamington Spa/New York: Berg.

Rodger, J. J. (2000) *From a Welfare State to a Welfare Society: The Changing Context of Social Policy in a Postmodern Era*, Basingstoke: Macmillan.

Room, G. (1979) *The Sociology of Welfare*, Oxford: Blackwell/Mott and Robertson.

Rose, R. (2006) *First European Quality of Life Survey: Participation in Civil Society*, Dublin: European Foundation for the Improvement of Living and Working Conditions.

Rose, R. and Newton, K. (2010) *Second European Quality of Life Survey: Evaluating the Quality of Society and Public Services*, Luxembourg: Office for Official Publications of the European Communities.

Rubington, E. and Weinberg, M. (eds.) (1981) *The Study of Social Problems: Five Perspectives*, 3rd edn, New York: Oxford University Press.

Rustin, M. and Chamberlayne, P. (2002) 'Introduction: From biography to social policy', in Chamberlayne, P., Rustin, M. and Wengraf, T. (eds.) *Biography and Social Exclusion in Europe Experiences and Life Journeys*, Bristol: Policy Press, pp. 1–21.

Rustin, M. and Rix, V. (1997) 'Anglo-Saxon individualism and its vicissitudes: Social exclusion in Britain', in Chamberlayne, P. (ed.) *Social Strategies in Risk Societies*, London: University of East London, SOSTRIS Working Paper 1, pp. 12–24.

Ryan, R. and Deci, E. L. (2001) 'On happiness and human potentials: A review of research on hedonic and eudaimonic well-being', *Annual Review of Psychology*, 52: 141–66.

Ryff, C. D. (1989) 'Happiness is everything, or is it? Explorations on the meaning of psychological well-being', *Journal of Personality and Social Psychology*, 57: 1069–81.

Ryner, M. (2010) 'An obituary for the Third Way', *Eurozine*, 27 April 2010.

Sainsbury, D. (1996) *Gender, Equality and Welfare States*, Cambridge: Cambridge University Press.

Saraceno, C. (2008) 'Patterns of family living in the enlarged Europe', in Alber, J., Fahey, T. and Saraceno, C. (eds.) *Handbook of Quality of Life in the Enlarged European Union*, London: Routledge, pp. 47–71.

Saraceno, C. and Negri, N. (1994) 'The changing Italian welfare state', *Journal of European Social Policy*, 4, 1: 19–34.

Saraceno, C., Olagnero, M. and Torrioni, P. (2005) *First European Quality of Life Survey: Families, Work and Social Networks*, Luxembourg: European Foundation for the Improvement of Living and Working Conditions.

Scheiwe, K. and Willekens, H. (eds.) (2009) *Child Care and Pre-school Development in Europe: Institutional Perspectives*, Basingstoke: Palgrave.

Searle, B. (2008) *Well-being*, Bristol: Policy Press.

Sen, A. (1984) *Resources, Values and Development*, Oxford: Basil Blackwell.

Sen, A. (1992) *Inequality Reexamined*, Oxford: Clarendon Press.

Sen, A. (1999) *Development as Freedom*, New York: Knopf.

Sevenhuijsen, S. (1998) *Citizenship and the Ethics of Care Feminist Considerations on Justice, Morality and Politics*, London: Routledge.

Silver, H. (1994) 'Social exclusion and social solidarity: Three paradigms', *International Labour Review*, 133, 5/6: 531–78.

Skocpol, T. (1995) *Protecting Soldiers and Mothers: The Political Origins of Social Policy in the United States*, Cambridge, MA: Harvard University Press.

Smith, D. E. (1993) 'What welfare theory hides', in Drover, G. and Kerans, P. (eds.) *New Approaches to Welfare Theory*, Aldershot: Edward Elgar, pp. 242–8.

Social Protection Committee (2009) *Growth, Jobs and Social Progress in the EU: A Contribution to the Evaluation of the Social Dimension of the Lisbon Strategy*, Brussels: European Commission.

Spicker, P. (1991) 'Solidarity', in Room, G. (ed.) *Towards a European Welfare State?*, Bristol: SAUS, pp. 17–37.

Spicker, P. (1997) 'Exclusion', *Journal of Common Market Studies*, 35, 1: 133–43.

Starke, P., Obinger, H. and Castles, F. G. (2008) 'Convergence towards where? In what ways, if any, are welfare states becoming more similar?', *Journal of European Public Policy*, 15, 7: 975–1000.

Stewart, K. (2009) 'Poverty, inequality and child well-being in international context: Still bottom of the pack?', in Hills, J., Sefton,

T. and Stewart, K. (eds.) *Towards a More Equal Society? Poverty, Inequality and Policy since 1997*, Bristol: Policy Press, pp. 267–90.

Stiglitz, J. A., Sen, A. and Fitoussi, J.-P. (2009) *Report by the Commission on the Measurement of Economic and Social Progress* (available at: www.stiglitz-sen-fitoussi.fr, accessed: 15 August 2010).

Sugden, R. (1993) 'Welfare, resources, and capabilities: A review of *Inequality Reexamined* by Amartya Sen', *Journal of Economic Literature*, 31: 1947–62.

Sum, A. and McLaughlin, J. (2010) *How the US Economic Output Recession of 2007–2009 led to the Great Recession in Labor Markets: The Role of Corporate Job Downsizing, Work Hour Reductions, Labor Productivity Gains, and Rising Corporate Profits*, Boston: Center for Labor Market Studies, Northeastern University.

Tawney, R. H. (1931) *Equality*, London: Unwin.

Taylor, C. (1989) *Sources of the Self*, Cambridge: Cambridge University Press.

Taylor, G. (2007) *Ideology and Welfare*, Basingstoke: Palgrave.

Teles, S. M. (1996) *Whose Welfare? AFDC and Elite Politics*, Lawrence, KA: University of Kansas Press.

Temple, W. (1941) *Citizen and Churchman*, London: Eyre and Spottiswoode.

Therborn, G. (2004) *Between Sex and Power: Family in the World 1900–2000*, London: Routledge.

Therborn, G. (2009) 'The killing fields of inequality', *Soundings*, 42, Summer: 20–32.

Titmuss, R. M. (1958) *Essays on the Welfare State*, London: Allen and Unwin.

Titmuss, R. M. (1963) 'The social division of welfare', in *Essays on the Welfare State*, London: Allen and Unwin, pp. 34–55.

Titmuss, R. M. (1974) *Social Policy: An Introduction*, London: Allen and Unwin.

Titmuss, R. M. (2001) 'The welfare state: Images and reality', in Alcock, P., Glennerster, H., Oakley, A. and Sinfield, A. (eds.) *Welfare and Wellbeing Richard Titmuss's Contribution to Social Policy*, Bristol: Policy Press, pp. 49–58.

Townsend, P. (1979) *Poverty in the UK*, Harmondsworth: Penguin.

Tronto, J. C. (1987) 'Beyond gender difference to a theory of care', *Signs*, 12, 4: 644–63.

Tronto, J. C. (1993) *Moral Boundaries. A Political Argument for an Ethic of Care*, London: Routledge.

Turner, B. (1993) *Citizenship and Social Theory*, London: Sage.

Turner, R. S. (2008) *Neo-liberal Ideology History, Concepts and Policies*, Edinburgh: Edinburgh University Press.

UNRISD (2010) *Why Care Matters for Social Development*, Research and Policy Brief 9, Geneva: UNRISD.

Van den Bosch, K. (2001) *Identifying the Poor*, Aldershot: Ashgate.

Van Kersbergen, K. (1995) *Social Capital: A Study of Christian Democracy and the Welfare State*, London: Routledge.

Van Oorschot, W. (2006) 'Culture and social policy: A developing field of study', *International Journal of Social Welfare*, 16: 129–39.

Veenhoven, R. (2007) 'Subjective measures of well-being', in McGillivray, M. (ed.) *Human Well-being: Concept and Measurement*, Basingstoke: Palgrave, pp. 214–39.

Wacquant, L. (2009) *Punishing the Poor: The Neoliberal Government of Social Insecurity*, Durham, NC: Duke University Press.

Walker, A. and Collins, C. (2004) 'Families of the poor', in Scott, J., Treas, J. and Richards, M. (eds.) *The Blackwell Companion to the Sociology of Families*, Oxford: Blackwell, pp. 193–217.

Walker, R. (2005) *Social Security and Welfare: Concepts and Comparisons*, Milton Keynes: Open University Press.

Walzer, M. (1990) 'The communitarian critique of liberalism', *Political Theory*, 18, 1: 6–23.

Waring, M. (1988) *If Women Counted: A New Feminist Economics*, San Francisco: Harper & Row.

Weale, A. (1978) *Equality and Social Policy*, London: Routledge & Kegan Paul.

Wennemo, I. (1994) *Sharing the Costs of Children: Studies on the Development of Family Support in the OECD Countries*, Stockholm: Swedish Institute for Social Research.

Western, B. (2006) *Punishment and Inequality in America*, New York: Russell Sage Foundation.

Whelan, C. T. and Maître, B. (2009) *Poverty and Deprivation in Ireland in Comparative Perspective*, Dublin: Economic and Social Research Institute.

White, S. and Ellison, M. (2007) 'Well-being, livelihoods and resources in social practice', in Gough, I. and McGregor, J. A. (eds.) *Wellbeing in Developing Countries: From Theory to Research*, Cambridge: Cambridge University Press, pp. 157–75.

Wiggan, J. (2010) 'Something Red, Bold and New? Welfare Reform and the Modern Conservative Party', paper presented to Social Policy Association Annual Conference, 5–7 July 2010, Lincoln.

Wilkinson, R. (1996) *Unhealthy Societies: The Afflictions of Inequality*, London: Routledge.

Wilkinson, R. and Pickett, K. (2009) *The Spirit Level: Why More Equal Societies Almost Always Do Better*, London: Allen Lane.

Wilkinson, W. (2007) In Pursuit of Happiness Research: Is it Reliable? What Does it Imply for Policy? *Cato Institute Policy Analysis*, 590, April 2007.

Williams, F. (1989) *Social Policy: A Critical Introduction*, Cambridge: Polity.

Williams, F. (1999) 'Good-enough principles for welfare', *Journal of Social Policy*, 28, 4: 667–87.

Williams, R. (1976) *Keywords: A Vocabulary of Culture and Society*, London: Fontana/Croom Helm.

Wilson, E. (1977) *Women and the Welfare State*, London: Routledge.

Woodward, A. and Kohli, M. (2001) 'European societies: Inclusions/exclusions?', in Kohli, M. and Woodward, A. (eds.) *Inclusions and Exclusions in European Societies*, London: Routledge, pp. 1–17.

Worts, D., Sacker, A. and McDonough, P. (2010) 'Re-assessing poverty dynamics and state protections in Britain and the US: The role of measurement error', *Social Indicators Research*, 97, 3: 419–38.

Yeates, N. (2004) 'Global care chains: Critical reflections and lines of enquiry', *International Feminist Journal of Politics*, 6, 3: 369–91.

Young, J. (2007) *The Vertigo of Late Modernity*, London: Sage.

Young, I. M. (2008) 'Structural injustice and the politics of difference', in Craig, G., Burchardt, T. and Gordon, D. (eds.) *Social Justice and Public Policy Seeking Fairness in Diverse Societies*, Bristol: Policy Press, pp. 77–104.

Index

Note: page numbers in italics denote tables, boxes or figures